T. F. TORRANCE IN PLAIN ENGLISH

STEPHEN D. MORRISON

BELOVED PUBLISHING · COLUMBUS, OH

Published by Beloved Publishing in Columbus, Ohio. Printed on demand through the publishing services of On Demand Publishing, LLC.

Printed in the United States of America, unless otherwise stated.

Paperback ISBN: 978-1-63174-168-5

eBook ISBN: 978-1-63174-167-8

Cover illustration and design copyright © 2017 Gordon Whitney Media

(www.GordonWhitneyMedia.com)

ACKNOWLEDGEMENTS:

I would like to express my sincerest gratitude to Marty Folsom, Gary Parrett, and Mark MacLeod for their valuable comments and editorial advice on an early edition of this book. I would also like to express thanks to my friend Gordon Whitney for his custom illustration and cover design, but most of all for his friendship.

My deepest love and gratitude belongs to my wife of five years, Ketlin, whom I adore. You are my constant source of inspiration, motivation, and delight.

CONTENTS

FOREWORD BY MARTY FOLSOM

Whether entering a great museum, preparing for surgery, or starting a new job, it is always beneficial to have a guide who knows the subject well to open your understanding in words and images that reveal the unknown.

Stephen D. Morrison provides this guidance as he introduces readers to one of the great theological minds of the twentieth century, Thomas F. Torrance. With a helpful balance of Torrance's texts, he prepares the table. He then brings in concise voices, masters of Torrance's theology, to clarify the key ideas. Finally, Morrison adds his own reflections on the journey of discovery; this is a book to ignite the passion of any person who is interested but daunted, who needs a place to start this unveiling process.

The chapters in this book provide a logical sequencing that begins at the beginning and helps you climb the stairs to enjoy the view. The sidebars provide glimpses of insight as to why these issues matter in gaining clarity as we search for language to inform our knowing of the living God revealed in Jesus.

This book echoes the faithfulness of Torrance to display the splendor of the grace of God seen in the faithfulness of Jesus Christ. In the end, we are invited by the Spirit to know the Abba of Jesus and participate in the life of the Triune God. Throughout, one hears good news that is facilitated by the scientific endeavor to understanding the Trinity as personal and present, and in response to enter a life of worship and wonder. May your reading invite you to become a pilgrim afresh, awakened to breathe in this joy into which we are called.

MARTY FOLSOM, PhD

REFORMATION DAY, 2017

INTRODUCTION

Thomas F. Torrance was the first "proper" theologian I ever read. I remember devouring *The Mediation of Christ* almost five years ago, and I will never forget what a profound impact it had on me. I owe Torrance a debt of gratitude for igniting in me a passion for theology that has grown only stronger with time. I returned to Torrance, in preparation for this book, with a broader scope and context. After I had finished the first book in this series, *Karl Barth in Plain English,* I knew Torrance would be next, but I wrongly imagined it would be simple to write about him having already read so much of his work. As I began reading (and re-reading), I quickly realized I had only before scratched the surface of Torrance's multi-faceted thought. I returned with fresh eyes and was overcome by the remarkably vast body of work he produced in his lifetime.

George Hunsinger once called Torrance "arguably the greatest Reformed theologian since Karl Barth." Torrance's steady theological output was far-reaching and profound, as Hunsinger further notes: "Besides the theologian, the ecumenist, and the church leader, there were at least three other Torrances: the translator, the interdisciplinary theologian, and the historian of doctrine [...] In breadth of learning, depth of scholarship, quality of output, ecumenical conviction, and devotion to the Nicene faith, theology and church will not soon see another like him" (*Participatio,* Vol. 1 2009, 11-2).

Without a doubt, Torrance's theology presents a unique challenge to anyone wanting to understand him. His interests were vast, including prolonged dedication to the philosophy of science, Patristic scholarship, John Calvin, Scottish theology, ecumenical dialogue, hermeneutics, and Karl Barth. He was a systematic thinker but never produced a "systematic theology" through which he might be neatly understood. He admitted agreement with the German idiom, "One of the greatest enemies of *Wahrheit* ('truth') is *Klarheit* ('clarity')" (ibid., 13). All these factors make him at once fascinating to study, exceedingly important for the Church today, but, nonetheless, quite challenging to read.

Andrew Purves accurately describes what it is like to read T. F. Torrance:

> Torrance is fecund, lengthy to the point of prolixity, and relentlessly intense and encyclopedic (and exhausting) in style. With Torrance we enter a world where the theologian is ferociously battling for the integrity and faithfulness of theology [...] With Torrance we enter a world of theological science (his image), of theology as *kata physin,* theology developed according to the nature of the subject of inquiry: God as Father, Son and Holy Spirit, given for our salvation and known through Jesus Christ. This theology is assertive and kerygmatic, abundant with confidence and conviction, prone to soaring flights of generality, yet with close attention to detail.
>
> — Exploring Christology and Atonement, 53

Reading Torrance is like a hearty burst of exercise; it is often exhausting, but I always feel better off because of it. Repentance, a "change of mind," is an important aspect of Torrance's thought, and I have often found myself being forced to re-think my thinking on account of his insights. Torrance wrote like a scientist presenting a lab report, carefully and precisely showing us the data and its relevant conclusions. He has been rightly called a "theologian's theologian." His theology is often highly specialized. Although, this does not detract from the profound *practicality* of his thought. For Torrance, "All true theology is intensely practical" (*Theology in Reconstruction*, 26). While he may spend hundreds of pages on the epistemological implications of modern scientific thought for theology today, he nonetheless brings it all to the point of evangelical witness to the love and grace of God. His theology seamlessly moves from technically complex to profoundly practical, even doxological, in a matter of pages.

One of the greatest difficulties I came against in writing this book, beyond the actual work of reading Torrance, was deciding how to organize it. I drafted and revised no fewer than eight outlines before finally settling on the one you have before you today. But I am still not entirely satisfied with it. Torrance's thoughts on any given subject are spread across a wide number of books and essays, each with their own particular context. His work is difficult, if not impossible, to neatly summarize. How could I hope to offer any sort of cohesive overview of his thoroughly complex theology?

What I have settled on here is neither a perfect representation of Torrance's theology nor is it necessarily a flawed one. Instead, I structured this book according to the ideas I have found the most helpful for understanding Torrance. I do not attempt to present here a coherent, systematic summary of his *entire* theology. Instead, what you have before you is an honest attempt to understand Torrance in my own way, or, if you like, "in plain English." What you have before you articulates how I have personally come to grips with Torrance's densely complex thought, and I hope it serves as a helpful guide to you as well.

AN OUTLINE

This book consists of nine chapters, each emphasizing a selected "major idea" from Torrance's thought. Various "sidebars" follow each chapter, and these serve to address a controversial issue, make an important clarification, or pull out the practical implications from the chapter. These sections are for clarity and further dialogue.

The entire book is *loosely* broken up into two parts. The first part addresses Torrance's "scientific" interests, such as his engagement with natural science and his reformulated natural theology. This makes up the first three chapters. The second part addresses Torrance's more "evangelical" interests, such as the doctrine of the Trinity, the vicarious humanity of Christ, and the atonement. This makes up the final six chapters. These two parts are not a strict division, because Torrance's theology is never so neatly divided, but this was nevertheless a helpful way for me to organize this book.

I wrote this book as a crescendo of sorts, gradually building up to what I consider to be the capstone of Torrance's theology. It will be helpful to keep this progression in mind, especially when you are reading the earlier chapters, which can seem, at times, quite abstract without the chapters that come later. If you struggle with these, it is acceptable to skip ahead and circle back around.

With that said, here are the nine "major ideas" I have chosen to focus on in this book:

1. A "scientific" approach to theology, or "theological science."
2. Knowing reality *according to* the nature of the reality known (*kata physin*).
3. A reformulated (or "new") natural theology contextualized *within* divine revelation.
4. The oneness in being and act of the Father, Son, and Holy Spirit (*homoousion*).

5. The doctrine of the Trinity as the "ground and grammar" of theology.
6. The twofold agency (mediation) of Christ.
7. The vicarious humanity of Christ, or Christ's saving *life*.
8. The doctrine of the atonement, with an emphasis on its "threefold" nature.
9. "With Jesus besides God." Union with Christ and participation in the Triune God (*theosis*) as the capstone of Torrance's theology.

Eternal beginners

I am honored you have picked up my little book on Torrance. I was humbled by all of the positive responses to my first book in this series, *Karl Barth in Plain English*, and I hope this study of Torrance's thought is just as helpful and rewarding to read as that one was. I hope you are challenged, provoked, and inspired by looking into some of the important insights Torrance has to offer the Church today. Like my first book, this book was written from one amateur to another—it is yet again *for beginners, by a beginner*. Truly, in the communion of the Spirit, there are no "experts" before God, but only eternal beginners stupefied before God's indescribable wonder.

I hope you put down this book with a renewed awareness of the beauty of God's grace and love because I hope you understand that this book is not *primarily* about T. F. Torrance. This book is about the goodness and glory of God, and about how we might come to know God better in conversation with Torrance's profound theological contributions. So may we be ever more in awe of God's amazing grace, as we joyously participate, by the Spirit, in the Son's loving communion with the Father.

Stephen D. Morrison
Lund, 2017

BIOGRAPHY

Thomas Forsyth Torrance was born into a missionary family on August 30, 1913, in Chengdu, China. He died at the age of 94 on December 2, 2007, in Edinburgh. His life was characterized by his devout service to God, his passion for ministering the Gospel to all people, and by a staggering academic output of books, essays, lectures, and sermons. Alister McGrath writes, "Torrance's list of published works contain[s] roughly 320 works which originated during his twenty-nine year period as a professor at Edinburgh. Since retiring from that position in 1979, he has added a further 290 items, including some of his most significant works" (*T.F. Torrance,* 107). Without a doubt, Thomas F. Torrance was one of the most productive and passionate theologians of the last hundred years.

His parents were devout in their faith and passed on their deep love for God to all their children (each of whom would become, in one way or another, ministers of the Gospel). His father, also named Thomas Torrance, was a missionary to Western China. He was in charge of the American Bible Society for twenty-five years and was credited with distributing several million Bibles to the Chinese people. David Torrance (Thomas' younger brother) had this to say about their father's missionary efforts: "On his retirement in 1935 the churches said of him that no one had done more to take the Gospel to West China" (*The Promise of Trinitarian Theology*, 3).

As a young man, Torrance was inspired by his father's efforts. He hoped to one day follow in his footsteps and become a missionary to the Tibetan people. Torrance never became a missionary in the classical sense, but, as he wrote later in life, "I have remained a missionary at heart, and have regarded my theological work as a form of missionary activity" (ibid., 304). Torrance was a missionary to the academy. "He integrated his call for evangelistic work with a vocation to preach, first and foremost, to theologians!" (David W. Torrance, *Participato*, Vol. 1 2009, 27).

It was his family's immensely faith-filled environment that likely had such a dramatic impact on Torrance's thinking. The Torrance household met daily for worship and prayer, with a Bible study led by their mother. Although his father was the missionary of the family, Torrance considered his mother, Annie Elizabeth Torrance, to be the household theologian. John Calvin was a name commonly spoken in their home, and his mother often encouraged the family to read theological classics such as Luther's *Commentary on Galatians*. In fact, it was Torrance's mother who helped introduce him to one of his most important theological influences, Karl Barth. Before leaving for New College in Edinburgh, she gave him a copy of Barth's *Credo*.

It was in Edinburgh that Torrance came in contact with two more important theological influences: Hugh Ross Mackintosh and Daniel Lamont. Mackintosh especially was a consistent voice for the evangelical nature of Christian theology, and he gave a central place to the atoning work of Christ.

In 1937-38, after learning German in Berlin for a summer, Torrance went on to study with Karl Barth for his doctorate. Barth highly regarded Torrance and included him in a sort of "inner circle" of students who would meet once a week at his home. David Torrance insightfully reveals just how highly Barth thought of his brother, claiming he understood his theology better than anyone: "Barth wrote to him to say that of all his students and readers Tom was the one who understood him best" (*The Promise of Trinitarian Theology*, 24). When Barth eventually retired from his position at the university, he considered Torrance an ideal successor to take his place. But Torrance eventually declined the offer for his family's sake.

Torrance was set to write his dissertation on the doctrine of grace in the second-century Fathers but was unable to finish it until 1946. He intended to complete his doctorate in 1939, but he was recommended by John Baillie to teach systematic theology at Auburn Theological Seminary in New York (at the young age of 26). He took up the appointment, though it was short-lived. However, these early lectures laid much of the groundwork for his later theology, such as his pursuit of "scientific" theology, and his insistence that the person and work of Jesus Christ cannot be separated. (A selection from these lectures can be found in his book, *The Doctrine of Jesus Christ*.)

In the summer of 1939, Torrance returned to the U.K. because of the impending threat of war. Torrance applied to be an army chaplain, but his application was rejected due to lack of experience. He decided instead to continue work on his dissertation. Returning to Basel would have been impossible, so Torrance registered at Oriel College, Oxford. Although this was an intellectually stimulating time for Torrance, he felt it was inappropriate to continue his studies when so many parishes were left without pastors, since many were sent to war as chaplains. Torrance sought out a parish and was assigned to Alyth Barony Parish Church in March 1940. Three years later Torrance again applied to serve in the British army and was accepted through the Church of Scotland's Committee on Huts and Canteen Work for H.M. Forces, which supplied chaplains for both pastoral care and practical service.

Torrance narrowly escaped death on many occasions during the war. This constant danger was by his own choice, however, since he purposefully picked those positions which were nearest to the front of the battle. When the war ended in 1945, David Torrance recalls a letter he received from his brother, in which, "He was overwhelmed with the fact that he was still alive, and even uninjured, in light of all that he had experienced. He believed that again and again God had given him courage and sustained him in the face of death and destruction" (*The Promise of Trinitarian Theology*, 17).

After the war, Torrance returned to his parish in Alyth and set his attention on completing his dissertation. He received his doctorate *magna cum laude* in 1946.

Torrance's deep concern for the Church of Scotland was evident during this time. He founded the Scottish Church Theology Society in 1945, launched the *Scottish Journal of Theology* in 1948, and he jointly founded the Society for the Study of Theology in 1952. Torrance married Margaret Edith Spear in October 1946. He would often say getting married and having children was the best thing he ever did in life.

Torrance was appointed to a professorship at New College in 1950. He was initially assigned to teach Church history but was later assigned to the chair of Christian Dogmatics (1952). He taught on many subjects, especially Christology and soteriology (the doctrines of Christ and salvation), but was unable to lecture on the doctrine of God except to postgraduates. This was due to the way that the theology faculty (Divinity School) was organized at the time. After his retirement in 1979, however, he published two of his most important books on the doctrine of God: *The Trinitarian Faith* (1988) and *The Christian Doctrine of God, One Being Three Persons* (1996).

He was heavily engaged in the ecumenical movement. His most notable contribution was a joint agreement on the doctrine of the Trinity, which he spearheaded between the World Alliance of Reformed Churches and the Greek Orthodox Church. The agreement was reached in Geneva on March 13, 1991. It remains a significant achievement for continued ecumenical dialogue.

Torrance's life, much like his theology, was given over in faithful service to God. He was an inspiring individual, not only because of his vast theological contributions but also because of his sheer and unwavering dedication to preaching the Gospel of Jesus Christ. This dedication to the Gospel as truly good news of God's love and grace towards us is one of the central aspects of Torrance's theology as well as his life. Torrance was a true "evangelical" theologian. His life was one long witness to the love of God for all humanity poured out from the Father, through the Son, and in the Holy Spirit.

My favorite story from Torrance's life is one that highlights the evangelical quality of his work exceptionally well. This moving account comes from Torrance's unpublished memoir, *War Service: Middle East and Italy, 1943-5,* and was quoted in Alister E. McGrath's *T.F. Torrance: An Intellectual Biography.*

When daylight filtered through, I came across a young soldier (Private Philips), scarcely twenty years old, lying mortally wounded on the ground, who clearly had not long to live. As I knelt down and bent over him, he said: "Padre, is God really like Jesus?" I assured him that he was—the only God that there is, the God who had come to us in Jesus, shown his face to us, and poured out his love to us as our Saviour. As I prayed and commended him to the Lord Jesus, he passed away [...]

That incident left an indelible impression on me. I kept wondering afterwards what modern theology and the Churches had done to drive some kind of wedge between God and Jesus, and reflected on the damage done by natural theology to Christology and the proclamation of the Gospel! The evangelical teaching which I had from Karl Barth was considerably reinforced on the battlefield. There is no hidden God, no *Deus Absconditus,* no God behind the back of the Lord Jesus, but only the one Lord God who became incarnate in him. Years later in my Aberdeen parish an old lady who had not very long to live said to me one day: "Dr. Torrance, is God really like Jesus?" I was startled, for those were the very same words I had heard on that battlefield in Italy. What have we been doing in our preaching and teaching in the church, to damage in the faith of

our people the relation between their faith in Jesus Christ and God?
[...] That was the problem, a refracted or damaged relation between
Jesus and God, the hiddenness of God, which I found in Donald
Baillie's book, *God was In Christ,* in which he could only think out
the relation between God and Man in Christ as a paradox.

— War Service, 49-50; quoted in McGrath, 74

1

SCIENTIFIC THEOLOGY

SUMMARY: Torrance's work is marked by the rigorous pursuit of scientific theology. By the term "scientific," he means clear and precise knowledge, not impersonal or abstract. Scientific theology denotes a particular method for approaching the knowledge of God. This pursuit also necessitates a dialogue between theological science and the natural sciences, since Torrance thinks the theological and natural sciences are mutually indebted to—and dependent upon—one another.

IN TORRANCE'S OWN WORDS:

I do not believe that the Christian Church has anything to fear from the advance of science. Indeed, the more truly scientific inquiry discloses the structures of the created world, the more at home we Christians ought to be in it, for this is the creation which came into being through the Word of God and in which that Word has been made flesh in Jesus Christ our Lord. The more I engage in dialogue with scientists and understand the implications of their startling discoveries, the more I find that, far from contradicting the fundamental beliefs, they open up the whole field for a deeper grasp of the Christian doctrines of creation, incarnation, reconciliation, resurrection and not least the doctrine of the Holy Spirit.

— T. F. TORRANCE, AS CITED BY DAVID W. TORRANCE:
THE PROMISE OF TRINITARIAN THEOLOGY, 25

It is because theological science and natural science both operate within the same space-time structures of the created universe, which are the bearers of all our intelligible order, that theological interpretation and explanation cannot properly take place without constant dialogue with the natural sciences, if we are to remain faithful to God as the creative Source of all rational structure and order.

— SPACE, TIME AND RESURRECTION, 23

SECONDARY QUOTES:

Torrance is convinced there is a right way to *do* Christian theology, or as he preferred, dogmatics, and this right way is a *scientific* one.

— MYK HABETS: THEOLOGY IN TRANSPOSITION, 27

INTRODUCTION

Many today wrongfully suppose a "war" exists between science and belief in God. Any dialogue between natural science and theology has almost entirely been reduced to apologetics. Within such a fierce cultural divide, Torrance stands out as a shining example of what a fruitful dialogue with science might actually look like in the modern world. If the Church today would follow Torrance's example, instead of militantly attacking the scientific perspective as if it were an enemy, then we might learn to see ourselves rightly as *allies* in a common pursuit. The Church needs to forge a new partnership with natural science, and Torrance's theology stands out as a valuable resource not often taken seriously enough.

This chapter serves as an introduction to some of the key aspects of Torrance's pursuit of scientific theology. Torrance spent a bulk of his career dedicated to this pursuit, but we will focus here only on its most notable aspects. I will first explain what Torrance does and does not mean by using the term "science," and then we will discuss the dialogue Torrance finds essential to both natural science and theology.

The first three chapters of this book are somewhat technical, as Torrance's scientific theology is certainly a challenge to understand. If this chapter and the two that follow it become a burden to read, then you have my permission to skip them and return later. After grasping more of Torrance's theology you may be able to return with better clarity. Ideally, however, I hope you decide to challenge yourself by tackling this difficult aspect of Torrance's thought first before moving on to the more familiar territory.

WHAT DOES TORRANCE MEAN BY "SCIENCE"?

When people think of the term "science," they typically imagine a particular *kind* of science, usually a natural science such as biology or astronomy. However, for Torrance, science is a technical term concerning the *way* we acquire knowledge, whether that is knowledge of the universe of space and time, the biology of mammals, or even in seeking the knowledge of God. Each subject may be pursued scientifically. This is why Torrance often talks about the "science of God," or "theological science." This is not to imply that Torrance studies natural science as a way leading up to God—as if God might be found in the heavens through a telescope. No, Torrance is firmly dedicated to God's self-revelation, Jesus Christ. He does not abandon revelation in the pursuit of scientific theology. In fact, the opposite is true. Torrance is more dedicated to God's self-revelation *because* of his conviction that theology must be scientific.

Clarifying what Torrance means when he talks about science will be helpful as we begin to explore the scientific aspect of his thought. While he does often engage with natural science, it would be a mistake to think Torrance is not properly a theologian of the Word of God. Torrance explains this well:

> There are not two ways of knowing, a scientific way and a theological way [...] Indeed because there is only one basic way of knowing we cannot contrast science and theology, but only natural science and theological science, or social science and theological science. In each we have to do with a fundamental act of knowing, not essentially different from real knowing in any field of human experience. Science is the rigorous and disciplined extension of that basic way of knowing and as such applies to every area of human life and thought. It should be clear, then, that I am not using 'science' in the vulgar sense to mean only natural science [...] I am using 'science' to denote the critical and controlled extension of our basic modes of rational activity with a view to positive knowledge.
>
> — GOD AND RATIONALITY, 91-2

Scientific inquiry, for Torrance, is not limited to a particular *kind* of science, which explains why he often called theology a science (even if few people today think of it as a science). If you define science the way some commonly do, with exclusive reference to physics, biology, or astronomy, then you miss Torrance's point. Torrance is seeking a scientific way of thinking about God, a scientific method of knowing God in accordance with God's nature. The pursuit of a scientific investigation into reality is not exclusive to theology. In fact, there are parallels between the ways natural scientists investigate the created universe and the ways theological "scientists" (theologians) investigate the reality of God known through the incarnate life of Jesus Christ. Thus, in plain terms, Torrance defines science as "nothing more or less than clear, precise knowledge" (ibid., 114).

Scientific thinking is more about *how* we know than it is about *what* we know. Although, as Torrance often points out, what we know should always dictate how we know it (*kata physin,* see chapter two). This leads us to consider a critical distinction Torrance makes between natural and theological science. While both sciences share a dedication to an accurate knowledge of reality, the way that natural science and theological science each pursue their respective realities (either the world or God) is unique to their task.

Natural science *discovers* the knowledge of reality through its investigations and studies. In contrast, theological science is grasped by its sovereign Subject, that is, it is *confronted* by divine revelation. Theology is chiefly concerned with God's Word made flesh in the incarnate life of Jesus Christ. We do not question God but *are questioned* by God. We are confronted by God's self-revelation in the person of Jesus Christ; we do not discover God in our own strength or through our own isolated observations. Theological science is therefore impossible if God has not first spoken to us. Nature, on the contrary, is mute and cannot speak for itself. Natural science *discovers* truth; theological science is *encountered by* the Truth.

This distinction helps us clarify a bit more of what Torrance has in mind with the pursuit of "scientific theology." Both sciences, natural and theological, pursue objective reality, but each pursuit is shaped by the nature of its object. Natural science pursues its object in a way that is different from theological science, even though both are rightly called a scientific pursuit.

Another misconception Torrance works to overcome is the notion that scientific knowledge is *impersonal* knowledge. Pure objectivity, that is, an impersonal knowledge of reality, is simply an illusion. We are unavoidably personal subjects who come to know reality subjectively. This, however, is precisely what people tend to think of when they imagine a scientific investigation. We may imagine science as a cold and impersonal pursuit of knowledge, in which the individual remains unaffected by reality, but the truth is we cannot escape ourselves. Scientific knowledge is therefore inherently *personal* knowledge.

Torrance sometimes refers to this impersonalization of science as a dualism between "theoretical and empirical aspects of reality" (*Christian Theology and Scientific Culture*, 23). With this Torrance means a divide between what we know in theory, or by pure reason, and what we know in practice, or through personal observation and interaction. Torrance considers this divide a *false* dualism that we must overcome in order to be truly scientific in our thinking. In fact, Torrance thinks this perspective has already been made obsolete in the world of natural science.

Following the insights of three important thinkers, Michael Polanyi, James Clerk Maxwell, and Albert Einstein, Torrance notes a movement of thought away from this divided outlook towards a more unified outlook. Science has moved beyond the false dualism of pure objectivity vs. pure subjectivity, and now understands that both objectivity and subjectivity work together in the pursuit of knowledge. Only a personal subject can distinguish their knowledge of reality from reality itself, their subjective knowledge of an object from the object of their knowledge, and so scientific objectivity *needs* subjective persons to be truly objective (and vice versa).

This insight is especially relevant for theology. To know God means to be personally reconciled to God in Jesus Christ. It is only as we come into a saving relationship with Christ and participate, in union with Him, in the life of the Triune God that we can apprehend knowledge of what God is like. We cannot do theology in a vacuum. Any definition of science as an impersonal pursuit is false. Both the natural and theological sciences depend on personal engagement with reality.

THREE AREAS OF OVERLAP AND DIALOGUE

Torrance argues that an "epistemological" dialogue is necessary between natural and theological science. (Epistemology denotes the theory of how we obtain knowledge.) We have already seen some of the overlap between natural and theological science in how each rejects the notion of an impersonal, dualistic pursuit of knowledge. Here we will continue to examine the three major areas of overlap that Torrance highlights between the two sciences. These are certainly not the only three areas of overlap, as Torrance's thought readily invites us to continue the dialogue, but these are the primary three Torrance himself addressed.

(I owe a debt to P. Mark Achtemeier for the precise terminology to describe these. See his essay "Natural Science and Christian Faith" in *The Promise of Trinitarian Theology*, 269-302.)

The first overlap is the *formal methodological*. We will discuss this at much greater length in the next chapter, but Torrance often adopts the Greek phrase *kata physin* to illustrate an important principle for the pursuit of knowledge, which is simply this: we know a reality scientifically only if we know it in accordance with itself. Therefore, both natural and theological sciences are supremely interested in developing a *mind* appropriate to reality. A natural scientist must learn to think in accordance with the aspect of nature they are working to discover, and the theologian must learn to think in accordance with God's self-revelation, Jesus Christ. This involves critically stripping our minds free from any foreign, *a priori* (theoretical), notions which have not derived directly in accordance with the reality we seek to know.

This is the *formal method* for the pursuit of knowledge that both the natural and theological sciences share, as Achtemeier notes:

> What theological and natural science do share methodologically is a common commitment to disciplined investigation and a common need for thought structures and habits of mind that mediate a true and undistorted encounter with the reality that constitutes their

respective fields of inquiry. Theological and natural science are thus both keenly interested in developing the *mind adequate to its object* —in purifying the active concepts that form the matrix of their encounter with the reality under investigation, and in identifying and eliminating distorting impositions of alien thought patterns that derive from outside sources.

— THE PROMISE OF TRINITARIAN THEOLOGY, 271-2

In other words, both sciences seek to know their object in accordance with its nature, and therefore, both sciences must critically undergo the elimination of any foreign ways of thinking that are not adequate to the nature of what they seek to know. Simply, we must *listen* to reality and learn from it; we must not project our own thoughts onto reality.

Therefore, Torrance is often called a "critical realist." This denotes an approach to reality that is mindful of both our *ability* to apprehend the truth of reality and our *inability* to apprehend its truth without critically developing a mind appropriate to its nature. This means that knowledge of reality is *possible* but not *automatic*. We can know reality, but we cannot know reality without first critically examining our inherent modes of thought. In this way, natural science and theological science share an essential formal method.

This is further explained by Torrance's consistent claim that proper scientific thinking must remain *open* to reality in order to be told what we could not have already told ourselves. If we learn what we already knew beforehand from our so-called "scientific" investigations, then it is likely we are not being properly scientific at all. Instead, it is far more likely we are projecting our former ways of thinking onto what we seek to know and interpreting reality in the light of our presuppositions.

Think of this in terms of theology. If our doctrine of God looks far too much like us—if God acts like us, thinks just like us, and does not truly *surprise* us from time to time—then perhaps we have conformed

God to *our* image. Scientific theology pursues knowledge of the living God, the God who is beyond our control, and therefore, scientific theology must reject all presuppositions and alien ways of thinking that do not derive from how God has actually been revealed to us in Jesus Christ. We must not conform God to *our* thinking but adjust our thinking to align with the truth of God's self-revelation.

The second overlap is in the shared *material interests* of both natural and theological science. This is primarily their mutual concern for the doctrine of creation. Both natural science and theological science have a keen interest in rightly understanding the world that God has made, and although they have different goals in mind, they nevertheless share this common pursuit.

Torrance thinks natural science especially owes a debt to theology for providing an understanding of the universe that made its science possible. In the ancient world, there was no sufficient cosmology to support a scientific understanding of the universe prior to the influence of Christian theology. The universe was believed to be eternal, closed, irrational, and therefore, *unknowable*. Within this understanding of the universe, natural science was impossible. Christian theology, in contrast, understood the universe as contingent, free, open, rational, and therefore, *knowable*. This was on account of the doctrine of creation out of nothing (*creatio ex nihilo*) thought together with the incarnation, which refuted the ancient, anti-scientific cosmologies that were commonly held. The inherent rationality of the universe (the belief that reality will make rational sense, that it may be known by us) is something we often take for granted, but Torrance thinks this simple change made scientific knowledge of the universe possible.

Christian theology, therefore, built the foundation upon which *all* scientific knowledge of the universe rests. In this sense, without the influence of Christian theology, the very pursuit of natural science would not have been feasible until perhaps much later in history. Christian theology was instrumental for natural science to break out of its cosmological prison.

However, as we will soon see, this dialogue was not wholly one-sided. Theology also owes a debt to natural science for helping it escape its own dualistic prison. Torrance thinks this shared interest in a proper understanding of the universe remains mutually beneficial for both natural and theological science today.

A key element of this material overlap, for theology, is Torrance's conviction that we cannot speak of our relation to God in terms of merely God and humanity, but must speak of a relationship between God/universe/humanity. There must be a consideration of the created world included in our theological thinking. We do not exist in a vacuum but are creatures of space and time who exist in the created universe. Therefore, theology should not be reduced to merely the consideration of the God/human relation, but it must consider the relation of God with human beings who exist within the created order. Science helps us clarify more precisely the nature of God's creation, and therefore, it frees theology from false dualistic cosmologies. We will see an example of this in the next overlap.

The third and final place for dialogue is in the overlapping *historical developments* of both sciences. Torrance's conviction is that the natural and theological sciences have developed on a parallel course, although not always an identical one, because both sciences exist in the created order and share a mutual methodology. The history of natural and theological science is thus a *shared* history. Here we will see the outworking of the first and second areas of overlap. Since both sciences 1) share a method and 2) share a subject, then 3) they often develop in a complementary manner.

An example Torrance often uses is to contrast the cosmology of Newton against the cosmology of Einstein (according to his theories of general and particular relativity). While this history is far too complex for a simple summary, I do want to briefly highlight the major developments Torrance thinks took place between these two thinkers and how they directly overlapped with historical developments in Christian theology. Keep in mind that this is a minimalist summary of a complex history and many details are missing.

Newton's rigid science led to a highly "deistic" view of creation, in which the universe came to resemble a mechanical clock. Within such a universe, God was seen as the cosmic clock-maker who set it all in motion but who no longer interacts with its closed system.

As a result, Christian theology became deistic and deterministic in its thinking. That is, God was seen both as the "far off" God (deistic) and as the God who "pre-determined all things" (deterministic). This can be seen quite clearly in the medieval doctrine of God as an "Unmoved Mover" (taken over from Aristotle), but also in the development of an independent natural theology, which sought out a logical bridge between the world and God. Newton himself doubted the incarnation, favoring Arius over Athanasius, because, according to his cosmology, God *cannot* be involved in our closed universe. Notions of God as the primal "First Cause" can also be seen at play here in the theological thinking that resulted from Newton's cosmological outlook. God was thought of strictly in terms of causal relations and not in terms of how He has actually interacted with us in the person and work of Jesus Christ. This tended to "philosophicalize" theology, as seen for example in the great *Summa Theologica* of Thomas Aquinas.

Achemeier again offers a helpful summary:

> In short, the Newtonian worldview is quite hostile to the Nicene [early Christian] understanding of the universe. The contingence and open-endedness of creation in Nicene understanding tends to be swallowed up in the mechanistic determinism and reductionism which are characteristic of the Newtonian outlook.
>
> — THE PROMISE OF TRINITARIAN THEOLOGY, 286

Natural science, however, did not remain trapped in this Newtonian outlook, nor did theological science remain trapped in its deterministic, deistic, and dualistic tendencies. Torrance most often discusses the work of Albert Einstein and Karl Barth for enacting this shift in thought (though not *only* these two).

Einstein's theories of special and general relativity effectively undid the Newtonian understanding of space and time as mechanistic and rigid. Einstein saw the dynamic interrelatedness of all reality, thus overthrowing Newton's tendency to separate reality into isolated parts like a mechanical clock. For Einstein, space and time were not fixed and static realities but dynamic, fluid, and relational. This cleared the way for an understanding of creation as open, contingent, free, and rational.

This also initiated a return to a theology more fully Nicene in nature. Especially in the work of Karl Barth, one of Torrance's greatest theological influences, freedom from Newtonian science meant a new, relational understanding of God's interactions with the world, a return to the importance of the incarnation, and a more dynamic under-standing of God's acts in Jesus Christ. The rejection of philosophical speculation regarding God's nature, along with the rejection of all independent forms of natural theology, characterized Barth's theolog-ical program. In Barth's work, Torrance saw the means for a truly "sci-entific" theology, a theology that does not develop abstract, philosophical constructions of God's nature, but thinks and speaks strictly in accordance with God's self-revelation, Jesus Christ.

Torrance writes about this movement of thought from many different angles, but the Newtonian and Einsteinian development seems to be the most predominant, which is why I have chosen this example to explain the historical overlap. It can be more generally understood as a movement from a divided and mechanical view of the universe towards a unified and relational understanding. Both the natural and theological sciences have benefited from this historical development.

NATURAL SCIENCE AND THE PRAISE OF CREATION

With all this in mind, it now should make sense why Torrance claims "natural science and theological science are not opponents but partners before God" (*The Ground and Grammar of Theology,* 7). For Torrance, natural science has the special task of articulating the praises of creation towards its Creator. Since the created universe is mute and cannot speak for itself, Torrance thinks that natural science, whether it acknowledges it or not, proclaims the wonders and glory of God in discovering the mysteries of creation. Because of this, Torrance often called the natural scientist a "priest of creation," writing:

It is man's function to bring nature to word, to articulate its dumb rationality in all its latent wonder and beauty and thus to lead the creation in its praise and glorification of God the Creator. That is, as I have called it, the priestly function of man to the creation, within which scientific inquiry becomes an authentically religious duty in man's relationship with God.

— REALITY AND SCIENTIFIC THEOLOGY, 69

Without man, nature is dumb, but it is man's part to give it word: to be its mouth through which the whole universe gives voice to the glory and majesty of the living God.

— THE GROUND AND GRAMMAR OF THEOLOGY, 6

The relationship between natural and theological science, far from being a hostile relationship, is one of co-dependence and mutual benefit. Theological science needs natural science and natural science needs theological science.

WHY DOES THEOLOGY NEED NATURAL SCIENCE?

In clarifying and critically sharpening the forms of thought through which we investigate reality, natural science frees theology from becoming an *ideology*. Without critically examining our *minds*, or the rationality through which we seek to know God, we will fail to properly speak of God at all. We will remain in a subjective prison, only speaking of God by speaking of *ourselves* in an elevated tone. Torrance writes:

> This dialogue with pure science can do theology nothing but good, for it will help theologians to clarify their fundamental methods in the light of their own peculiar subject-matter, and to wrestle again with the implacable objectivity of the Word of God until they learn to distinguish objective realities more clearly from their own subjective states.
>
> — THEOLOGY IN RECONSTRUCTION, 17

Torrance thinks theology can break free from the limits of a purely "subjective" knowledge of God through an epistemological dialogue with the natural sciences. Theology must learn to integrate personal knowledge within the pursuit of the objective reality that (or more properly Whom) we seek to know. (We will discuss this integration further in the next chapter.)

Furthermore, as we noted above, theology needs natural science because theology takes place within the creaturely world of space and time and not without it. Theology does not occur in the relation of timeless, spaceless human beings and God, but of human beings *within the cosmos* of space and time. Theology simply cannot ignore the insights of natural science, because for better or for worse, theology is a science bound to this created order. Failing to learn from natural science will only be to the detriment of theology, and there are only benefits from continued engagement.

Why does natural science need theology?

Torrance approvingly quotes the philosopher John Macmurray, who claimed, "It was Christianity that gave us science by its insistence on the spirit of truth [...] Science is sustained by the love of the truth. Apart from a passionate belief in the supreme value of truth, and from the willingness to sacrifice pleasant illusions to that faith in the truth, the whole truth and nothing but the truth, science could neither begin nor continue" (*Freedom in the Modern World*, 33; cited in Torrance, *Theological Science*, 76). Torrance thinks it is here that "theology has made [a] significant contribution to the rise of modern science" (ibid., 75). He continues:

> In this event a theology faithful to its object is in a position to show other sciences the real meaning of objectivity, precisely because in theological science above all we have to do with an object that encounters us as the Lord and Master, who will not be subdued to the forms of our subjectivity, but who will be known only in His Lordship over us. It is this humility and submission of theological knowledge to the sheer master and objectivity of the Truth that can help to shed light upon every struggle for objectivity, and every attempt at scientific knowledge. Utter respect for objectivity is the *sine qua non* [absolute essential] for scientific activity.
>
> — IBID., 85

This respect for objectivity in theological knowledge is an important contribution to the development of natural science, according to Torrance, which we highlighted above with the historical debt natural science owes to Christian theology.

Another reason why natural science needs theology, one of increasing relevance for science today, has to do with the limitations of what a human can know about existence. Natural science is finding itself up against a "frontier" that it cannot bridge without the help of theology. In other words, natural science is coming to grips with the inevitable question of a "beyond," whether it takes the form of belief in a higher power, a cosmic force, or of the God and Father of Jesus Christ. Inevitably, natural science must admit its need for theology and faith, as Torrance writes:

> [S]cientists today frequently find themselves at the frontiers and limits of their science compelled to ask open questions directed toward an intelligible ground [God] beyond the determinations of science, but without which science would not ultimately be consistent or make sense. In other words, the more scientific inquiry presses toward the boundary conditions of intelligibility in the physical universe—whether in its microscopic or in its macroscopic aspects—the more scientists find themselves thrust up against the question of the creation and the Creator.
>
> — THE GROUND AND GRAMMAR OF THEOLOGY, 17-8

Natural science is facing questions that it can no longer answer within the sphere of the created world, questions that are forcing its gaze above this created order to its intelligible ground. In other words, natural science is discovering the necessity of theological reflection on the God who is the intelligible ground of all creation.

Torrance is clear here that this does not mean science has discovered proof of God, or that this could be used as an apologetic tool. No, for Torrance, this simply means that natural science is forced to admit there are some questions it faces that it can no longer adequately answer without turning to theology for help. Natural science depends on theological reflection to fill in the gaps in its knowledge of the universe, and it always will (whether it admits it or not). The idea that natural science does not need God is simply false since it will always depend on the inherent intelligibility of the universe, which is grounded on God's own intelligibility. Without God as its intelligible ground, the universe would be unknowable and irrational.

While our modern culture has divided faith from science, Torrance thinks science is finding its way back to faith by admitting the need for faith as an essential part of its science. Einstein is a good example, as he famously spoke of science invoking a kind of religious awe; we might also point to James Clerk Maxwell and Michael Polanyi since both scientists had a profound faith in God at the root of their discoveries. The cultural dualism between faith and science is falling apart on both sides of the divide. This means the old notion that science can operate without faith, without a fundamental awareness of a "beyond" lying past its frontier, is over. (Likewise, we should say the reverse: faith can no longer operate without the natural sciences.) Science needs theology to answer the questions it is finding it cannot answer alone because it has reached the limits of what is possible to learn in the observable universe. The theological and natural sciences working together can bring about a deeper understanding of the universe, together articulating the mute praise of creation to its Creator.

SIDEBAR: NON-DUALIST THOUGHT

"I believe that human thought is now in the midst of one of the greatest transitions of history, which we must take with the utmost seriousness" (*The Ground and Grammar of Theology*, ix). This is the movement of thought from *dualistic* ways of thinking to *unitary* or *holistic* ways of thinking about reality. Torrance argues that we cannot ignore the importance of this transition.

Already in this first chapter, we have encountered the term "dualism." What exactly does this mean? Simply, dualism denotes a way of thinking that fails to take reality into consideration as a unified whole and works with an inherently divided concept of reality instead. Torrance's thought is characterized by this dedication to a non-dualist (unitary/holistic) outlook. That is, Torrance strives to think in a *unified* way about reality so that no part is considered in isolation from the whole.

This rejection of dualism is part of what makes Torrance so difficult to read; it necessitates an entirely *new way of thinking* and not just new thoughts. It also explains why Torrance's theology was so profoundly interconnected. It caused him to think through every issue as part of the whole and not as a series of isolated considerations. For example, as we will discuss later in this book, Torrance insists that Christ's person and work cannot be separated, that Jesus and God cannot be divided, and that the life, death, resurrection, and ascension of Christ cannot be thought of properly except as a unified whole.

We should note, however, that Torrance's non-dualist perspective is not a systematic conclusion he assumes to be true *prior* to any engagement with reality itself. It is no pure theory applied abstractly to reality. Instead, this is a conclusion Torrance makes by thinking in accordance with reality, by allowing it to disclose itself to our thinking. So it is important not to mistake this non-dualist perspective with an *a priori* (theoretical) construction. It is only by thinking in accordance with reality that rejecting the dualist outlook becomes necessary.

Gary W. Deddo has rightly noted that "the significance of Torrance's contribution can only be fully grasped when one realizes that his theological formulations call for the cultivation of new habits of mind, new ways of thinking, not just new thoughts" (*The Promise of Trinitarian Theology*, 81). Torrance not only presents us with new ideas but an entirely new mindset. This manifests itself in many ways, from Torrance's doctrine of the Holy Spirit (the subject of Deddo's essay) to his non-dualist outlook. Here we will consider Torrance's uniquely non-dualist thought by examining the two major dualisms he argues against.

TWO FORMS OF DUALISM

There are two basic forms of dualism that Torrance finds severely problematic. The first is a *cosmological* dualism, and the second is an *epistemological* dualism; the first has to do with a divided universe and the second with a divided mind.

A *cosmological dualism* separates God from the world in a deistic, deterministic fashion, in which God either cannot or will not be personally involved in the universe. Here God is thought of as some far-away God, wholly indifferent to humanity. This refers back to the Newtonian cosmology, in which God is understood as a master clock-maker who merely set things in motion, but who is no longer actively involved in the world.

For Torrance, this dualism is ultimately overcome by thinking through the implications of the incarnation together with the doctrine of creation. God's becoming a human being in Jesus Christ, held together logically with the creation of the world out of nothing, brings an end to any false cosmology that denies God's interaction with the world. If we take the incarnation seriously, then we must reject the dualist idea that God is far removed from humanity, precisely because God became a human being in Jesus Christ. Therefore, God *is* profoundly involved in the world; God is no disinterested bystander.

Reminiscent of Athanasius' *On the Incarnation,* Torrance often wrote that it was the same God who created the world out of nothing who became a human in order to redeem our world, marred by sin, from falling back into nothingness. The incarnation revealed God's unwavering faithfulness to the human race. This connection between the creation and incarnation is, for Torrance, an important point for overcoming any such cosmological dualism.

An *epistemological dualism* separates empirical and theoretical knowledge, or in other words, knowledge of personal engagement and pure theory. Elmer Colyer writes, "Epistemological dualisms assert or presuppose a disjunction between the human knower and the reality that the human subject seeks to know" (*How to Read T.F. Torrance,* 58). As a result, knowledge is separated into two irreconcilable areas (the pure and the practical). We have already discussed this kind of dualism in the previous chapter.

This dualism is particularly damaging to our understanding of the universe by separating the knower from the reality they seek to know. If we give into this epistemological divide, we are forced to resign our knowledge of reality to pure subjectivity. We, in this dualist outlook, cannot know reality *as it actually is,* but are limited by our subjective perceptions and left to only apprehend reality *as it appears to us.*

An epistemological dualism of this magnitude results in utter irrationality. If we cannot know an object as it is in itself but only as it appears to us, then we are thrown back upon ourselves and have no scientific knowledge about the world at all. Much of this dualism can be traced back to the philosopher Immanuel Kant, whom Torrance is quite critical of in many of his books. Ultimately, Torrance feels natural science has *already* overcome Kant's epistemological dualism with its philosophy of science, and theology should learn from science how to overcome this split between the empirical and theoretical. Theology would be foolish to ignore how natural science has overcome this epistemological dualism.

Is God really like Jesus?

These two forms of dualism are not the only examples we could list from Torrance's thought, but they are the two most common ones. Torrance has also written on cultural and academic dualisms, such as the divide between the study of the "humanities" and the "sciences." However, the cosmological and epistemological dualisms are the primary points of view that Torrance argues we must reject.

There is, however, another significant dualism that we will return to later on in this book (in chapter four), which we might call a "theological" dualism. Though it is mostly the by-product of the cosmological dualism we described above, this dualism is one of the most problematic for Torrance. A theological dualism involves the wrongful division of the being and act of the Father from the being and act of the Son. Torrance's ultimate argument against dualistic ways of thinking is his emphasis on the Nicene doctrine of the *homoousion*, referring to the oneness in being, or consubstantiality, of the Father and the Son. This oneness in being and act is also extended to the Holy Spirit. We cannot think of any act or being of God the Father, the Son, or the Holy Spirit which is in any way divided, since God's being and act is always united, even in distinction. The doctrine of *homoousion* undoes this theological dualism.

Our biographical sketch of Torrance's life ended with his reflections about a dying soldier who asked with his final breaths, "Is God *really* like Jesus?" The question, repeated again by a parishioner in Scotland, reveals a much larger problem at the core of theology today. We tend to split apart the being and act of the Son from the Father, that is, to fall prey to this theological dualism. While it is unlikely we would ever deny that the Son and the Father are one in being and act, we far too often ignore this essential truth by pushing it to the peripheral of our thinking. As a result, there are many believers today who wrestle internally to reconcile two opposing images of God. (I know firsthand what this is like.) On the one hand they love and believe in Jesus Christ, the friend of sinners, the God of grace and mercy; but on the other hand, they *fear* His vengeful Father, the wrathful divine judge up in the sky keeping a list of all their wrongs in order to hold it against them. This divide is perhaps the most important dualism Torrance works to overcome, but we will return to examine it at a much greater length later.

2

KNOWLEDGE ACCORDING TO NATURE
(KATA PHYSIN)

SUMMARY: Central to Torrance's scientific theology is the conviction that true knowledge is knowledge *according to* the nature of the reality we seek to know. Reality itself must be free to determine how we know it, how we verify our knowledge of it, and what kind of rationality we understand it with. This is a sort of "epistemological repentance," designated by the Greek term *kata physin*.

IN TORRANCE'S OWN WORDS:

We can know God and speak about him truly only in accordance with his nature.

— THEOLOGY IN RECONSTRUCTION, 53

In any rigorous scientific inquiry you pursue your research in any field in such a way that you seek to let the nature of the field or the nature of the object, as it progressively becomes disclosed through interrogation, control how you know it, how you think about it, how you formulate your knowledge of it, and how you verify that knowledge. I often speak of this as *kataphysic inquiry,* a term that comes from the Greek... [meaning] 'according to nature.'

— PREACHING CHRIST TODAY, 45

SECONDARY QUOTES:

"The fundamental axiom that runs through all of Thomas F. Torrance's many publications on theological method is that the nature of the object or subject-matter in question defines the methods employed in investigating it, the mode of rationality used in conceptualizing what is discovered, and the form of verification consonant with it."

— ELMER E. COLYER: HOW TO READ T.F. TORRANCE,

322

INTRODUCTION

One of T.F. Torrance's chief theological concerns is the need for thinking and speaking in a manner worthy of God, that is, in a *godly* way. This is at the heart of his pursuit of scientific theology. In the previous chapter we introduced what Torrance means by the term "scientific," and we also sampled some of the fruits from his dialogue with natural science. A key aspect of this pursuit is Torrance's conviction that all authentic knowledge must be knowledge *in accordance with* the reality we seek to know. The nature of reality must be given control over our knowing of it, dictating how we know it, how we think and speak about it, and how we verify our knowledge of it. For this method, Torrance adopts the Greek term *kata physin.*

It has been helpful for me personally to equate this notion with the biblical call for repentance, or *metanoia,* which means a change of mind. There is evidence that Torrance makes this connection as well. The notion of *kata physin,* when applied to theological knowledge, calls us to repentance, to changing our minds in the light of Jesus Christ, and learning to think of God exclusively in terms of God's self-revelation.

KATA PHYSIN

Kata physin is a Greek phrase Torrance borrows from one of his most important Patristic influences, Saint Athanasius. It directly means "according to nature." It indicates Torrance's primary conviction regarding the proper method of theology, but also what he considers to be the fundamental method of *all* scientific inquiry, natural and theological alike. Torrance explains: "You know something only in accordance with its nature, and you develop your knowledge of it as you allow its nature to prescribe for you the mode of rationality appropriate to it" (*God and Rationality*, 52). Torrance then offers this (rather humorous) analogy:

> Thus I adopt toward another person quite a different mode of rationality from that which I adopt toward my desk, because his nature is different from that of a desk. Hence it would be quite irrational and unscientific to treat him like a block of wood or to treat the desk as if it were a human being. That is simple enough, but its implications are profound and far-reaching. Thus it would be utter nonsense for me to try to know God in the mode in which I know a creature or to treat Him as if He were a star. To know God, I must enter into the mode of rationality prescribed by the nature of God.
>
> — IBID.

We all would agree that approaching a human being as if they were a desk would be an act of utter irrationality, but far too often we adopt ways of approaching God which are equally irrational by not properly thinking in accordance with God's nature. A rational pursuit of God demands that we seek to know God *as God,* and accordingly, we must adopt a mind appropriate to divine revelation. We are required to *repent* of an irrational way of thinking, and to embrace a rational form of knowledge in accordance with God's self-disclosure. This is the essential conviction of *kata physin* within theological science.

For Torrance, this means we must develop the appropriate questions, questions asked in accordance with the nature and being of God, in order to receive truly *scientific* answers. This implies that there are inappropriate questions, or frames of thought, through which we might wrongly approach God. When we ask biological questions, we receive strictly biological answers, and when we ask economic questions, we receive economic answers. We do not receive philosophical, theological, or metaphysical answers from our biological or economical questions, and we rationally expect this to be the case. In the pursuit of scientific knowledge, our questions must be the *right kind* of questions, questions asked *in accordance* with the nature of the reality we question. Thus, Torrance writes:

> The progress of our science is the progress we achieve in asking questions. Genuinely scientific questions are questions that lead to new knowledge, questions that are open to the disclosure of what has not been known before.
>
> — IBID., 53

In order to learn something truly new about reality, we must learn it in accordance with its nature rather than subjecting reality to our own presupposed point of view. Accordingly, we must ask truly scientific questions. Our questions must *themselves* be questioned until they are made appropriate to the nature of our subject. Torrance notes that this is something tremendously difficult for us because we cannot separate ourselves from our questions. We *personally* must be changed by our inquiry.

I have found that the concept of *kata physin* is essentially a kind of *epistemological repentance.* Epistemology is the study of how we know, and repentance in the Greek means a change of mind (*metanoia*). In theology, to know God in accordance with God's nature means coming to repentance by personally engaging with God's self-revelation in Jesus Christ. Torrance makes this connection when he writes, "Scientific questioning reinforces the evangelical demand for repentance or *metanoia*, that is for an alteration in the basic structure of our mind" (*God and Rationality,* 119). Repentance is a key element in Torrance's thought because he is deeply concerned with pursuing truly *scientific* knowledge of God. Repentance is necessary in order to perceive reality rightly, to be free from alien forms of thought, and therefore, to come to know reality in accordance with its nature.

If theology is to be truly scientific in its knowledge of God, then theology cannot seek to know God primarily through philosophical speculation, apologetical proofs, or even by stringing together a series of out-of-context Bible verses. No, if theology is to be faithful in its pursuit of the knowledge of God, then theology must come to know God in accordance with God's very being and nature. This means taking up the "mind of Christ," and undergoing a "renewal of the mind" by the Holy Spirit and in union with Jesus Christ (1 Cor. 2:16, Rom. 12:2). This means giving God absolute sovereignty in our knowledge of God, thinking not with a center in ourselves but with a center in God's self-revelation. We know God only in accordance with God, that is, as the Son knows the Father and the Father knows the Son, and as we share together, by the Holy Spirit, in God's Triune self-knowing. God is not properly known by asking *human* questions in an attempt to speculate God's being apart from God's self-revelation. God is known only through God. God reveals Godself. From the Father, through the Son, and in the Holy Spirit we participate in the knowledge of God.

We will later examine this concept in a more directly Trinitarian context (chapter five), but for now, it is enough to note that *kata physin* is a fundamental and central conviction behind how Torrance pursues the knowledge of God. By way of a summary, then, Torrance writes of the theological need for a refined scientific method. Many of the themes we've discussed so far are restated here in this quotation, but it is important to see how Torrance now brings it all within its proper, evangelical context: the incarnation of Jesus Christ. The *mind of Christ* is essential for understanding *kata physin,* as Torrance writes at length:

> Perhaps the most difficult part of theology is the struggle we have with ourselves, with the habits of mind which we have formed uncritically or have acquired in some other field of knowledge and then seek with an arbitrary self-will to impose upon the subject-matter. We have to remind ourselves unceasingly that in our knowing of God, God always comes first, that in a genuine theology we do not think out of a centre in ourselves but out of a centre in God and his activity in grace towards us.
>
> Theology of this kind is possible only because God has already condescended to come to us, and has indeed laid hold of our humanity, dwelt in it and adapted it to himself. In Jesus Christ he has translated his divine Word into human form and lifted up our human mind to understand himself [...] We are driven back upon Jesus Christ as the proper ground for communion and speech with God. Because he is both the Word of God become Man and Man responding to that Word in utter faithfulness and truth, he is the Way that leads to the Father. It is in him and from him that we derive the basic forms of theological thinking that are appropriate both to divine revelation and human understanding.

— THEOLOGY IN RECONSTRUCTION, 9-10

LEVELS OF KNOWLEDGE ("STRATIFICATION")

Following Torrance's usage of *kata physin,* there is an important development in how we come to know God that we must now explore. This is what Torrance calls the "stratification" of knowledge, which identifies the levels of our knowledge of God.

Since every reality must be known only in accordance with its own nature, this leads to a way of thinking that is fundamentally *open* to reality. This acknowledges the essential control reality has over our knowledge of it and therefore accepts the open, stratified nature of that knowledge. We are not ourselves at the center of our knowledge, but that which we seek to know holds the controlling center of our thought. Therefore, Torrance insists that we must lay ourselves *open* to be told by reality the structure of its being, prescribing for us its own objectivity, since we cannot prescribe a *closed* objectivity to it. In other words, instead of forming a prior notion of what objectivity is, we must learn what it means to be objective in accordance with the reality we seek to know. This requires a fundamental *openness* to reality.

In contrast, a *closed* relationship with reality depends on a set of fundamental principles which exist independent of reality itself. Remaining open to reality necessitates that our statements are subject to change in relation to the disclosure of reality. The former becomes a self-contained, rigid, closed system, while the latter remains open and faithful to reality itself. Torrance's stratification of knowledge argues for an essentially open relation to reality, in contrast with a closed relation such as the kind we find in Christian fundamentalism.

Christian fundamentalism is a classic example of what happens whenever we attempt to *contain* reality with our statements rather than leave our statements *open* to being determined by reality itself. An "open" relation to reality gives priority to the truth over our understanding of it, thus leaving our understanding of reality subject to be changed by its truth, while a "closed" relation to reality gives a set of rigid statements priority over the truth of reality.

But what if natural science operated with the same sort of closed relationship to reality that fundamentalists do? What if, let us say, a group of astronomers worked with a set of closed fundamentals instead of maintaining an inherent openness to the universe? These astronomers would reject any new knowledge of the cosmos that contradicts their predetermined ideas about it. But could we accurately describe their method as *scientific*? Certainly not, since this would make astronomy a closed science rather than an open science. The openness of a science is necessary for its very existence. These astronomers would not be truly scientific in their pursuit, since they would no longer be concerned with reality as it is in itself, but have resigned themselves to focus on their own pre-established fundamental principles. This is the same error fundamentalism makes in Christian theology.

Christian theology must remain open to the knowledge of God rather than closed off by a rigid set of fundamentals. If we seek to truly know reality according to its own objectivity, then we must remain *open*, in repentance and humility, to be told what we could not tell ourselves, to learn new truths about reality. How much more must Christian theology, which pursues knowledge of the *living* God, avoid reducing God down to a set of rigid principles, than astronomy, which merely deals with created existence? We must remain open to God's reality if we are to be scientific in our knowledge of God and not closed off from the truth.

Benjamin Myers describes this openness well: "In true knowledge we are thus simultaneously involved in a movement of increasing openness to the object and in a subjective process of 'self-renunciation, repentance and change of mind.'" ("The Stratification of Knowledge in the Thought of T.F. Torrance," 3). This openness to reality is the other side of the coin of *kata physin*. We must remain open to reality, just as we must remove all foreign ways of thinking which do not conform to reality's inner rationality. We must repent from a false understanding of God, but we also must be careful to remain open to God's self-disclosure in Christ by the Holy Spirit.

Torrance then develops a theory of the "stratification" of knowledge on the basis of this openness to reality. This is not a presupposed model forced *onto* reality, but it is a *disclosure* model which arises by thinking in accordance with reality itself. In theology, this model develops into three stages, although Torrance admits there could theoretically be an infinite number of levels. The three stratified levels that Torrance names are the "evangelical and doxological level," the "theological level," and the "higher theological and scientific level" (*The Ground and Grammar of Theology*, 156-8). In simple terms, these are 1) the evangelical, 2) the theological, and 3) the scientific.

The strength of this theory is to unify knowledge gained through an empirical (practical/personal) encounter with a given reality together with the increasingly conceptual knowledge we scientifically develop as a result of continued engagement with reality. In other words, this model removes the false dualism between experiential knowledge and pure knowledge; we could also call this a dualism between the subjective and objective, or yet again the empirical and theoretical. Torrance develops this to show how the empirical must be integrated within the theoretical.

This all may seem rather technical at first, but as we begin to describe each level, especially as they unfold in the context of Christian theology, I hope it becomes more apparent what Torrance is describing. This theory is both simple and complex at the same time. It is likely something you have *already* done in your life many times over, although it's unlikely something you have ever had this precise terminology to describe.

1. Evangelical

The first level, the evangelical, Torrance describes as "the level of our day-to-day worship and meeting with God in response to the proclamation of the Gospel and the interpretation of the Holy Scriptures within the fellowship of the Church" (*The Ground and Grammar of Theology*, 156-7). From the first steps of our inquiry into the knowledge of God, Torrance rightly notes that the empirical and theoretical are woven together. Thus, "from the very start of our experience and knowledge, form and being, structure and substance, are indivisibly united in the realities with which we have to do and in our rational and experiential response to those realities" (ibid., 158).

This is the level of our personal encounter with God in the event of salvation, as well as in the continued life of a Christian in love, fellowship, and worship in community before God. Torrance notes that in these experiences with God we begin to apprehend the knowledge of God, even if we are unable to properly articulate it in a theological manner. Torrance often made the claim that we know more than we can express. For example, when Torrance writes, "A child by the age of five [...] has learned more 'physics' than he could ever bring to explicit understanding and expression even if he turned out to be a very brilliant physicist. We always know more than we can tell" (*Christian Theology and Scientific Culture,* 13). This is based on an "intuitive" reasoning which comes from personally encountering reality. At this stage, we have experienced God and have an indwelling knowledge of Him which we cannot yet properly express.

A good example from nature to explain this is in our experiences with hot and cold temperatures. A small child can walk outside and tell you if it is cold or warm, but as we grow up we learn to more precisely express what we already know intuitively, such as when we say on a hot day: "It is 85 degrees Fahrenheit." We already knew this with the term "hot," but we have moved into a new level of understanding with a more precise designation of temperature.

In our first and continued experiences with God through a loving and saving relationship with Jesus Christ—in the community of the Church by the Holy Spirit, and in personal devotion before God through prayer and scripture—we intuitively know more about God than we can express with any theological precision. This leads to the refinement of our knowledge of God in order to express more precisely (or explicitly) what we already know intuitively, and as a result, we are then able to better understand our personal experiences with God.

From this, we move to the next two levels, though it is without abandoning the first. For Torrance, all three levels are grounded on the third, on the innermost being and life of God. It is important to recognize this so we do not confuse these earlier levels with an attempt to build a theology upon any subjective basis. God remains the controlling center of all our theological knowledge, and it is only on this basis that we recognize the stratification of our knowledge.

2. THEOLOGICAL

In the second level, the theological, these experiences with God in salvation and communion lead us to consider the God whom we have experienced. This is quite natural. Think again of the analogy of a child intuitively recognizing hot and cold. After this child recognizes their awareness of hot and cold, they will become curious about these temperatures and wonder what causes them. This is what we do in this second level. We move from contemplating the experience to the reality experienced. We begin to articulate more precisely the knowledge of God by reflecting on God's self-revelation in God's acts towards us. This is what is often called the economic Trinity, or God for us. Torrance writes:

> As we direct our inquiries to God in this field [...] we find that he reveals himself to us as Father, Son, and Holy Spirit, in a three-fold movement of his love in revelation and redemption, in which we come up with certain basic concepts: that is, 'Father,' 'Son,' and 'Holy Spirit.'

> — THE GROUND AND GRAMMAR OF THEOLOGY, 158

In our personal encounter with God through salvation and communion, we come to know the revelation of God's acts as the Father, Son, and Holy Spirit. We have moved from experiencing God through salvation into a more precise knowledge of God in the acts of God for us. We go beyond contemplating what God has done *for me* into contemplating *who this God is* who has done this for me.

So far we have 1) God as experienced in our involvement in the Church and reading the Bible and 2) God as revealed for us in the person of Jesus who discloses His Father and gives us His Spirit. From this, we move to the third level, which ultimately grounds the first and the second.

3. Scientific

The third level, the scientific, is what Torrance calls the "higher theological and scientific level." In this, we move from the economic Trinity to the ontological Trinity, from God for us to God in Godself. Here we

> penetrate more deeply into the self-communication of God in the saving and revealing activity of Christ in his Spirit [...] This is the movement of thought in which we are compelled, under pressure from God's self-communication, to acknowledge that what God is toward us in the three-fold economic activity of his revelation and redemption, as Father, Son, and Holy Spirit, he is antecedently and eternally in his own Being in the Godhead.

> — The Ground and Grammar of Theology, 157-8

We are compelled to realize that who God is for us in Jesus Christ is who God is antecedently in Godself. We move from the external acts of God as Father, Son, and Holy Spirit to the *internal relations* of the Godhead. This is the high point of theological knowledge, in which we contemplate the very mystery of God's innermost being. This leads us to 3) know the depths of the love of God's life and to experience our inclusion in this communion of love.

Here Torrance closely connects theology with doxology (worship). Theology is, for Torrance, "rational worship" of God, in which we are profoundly oriented towards God in a posture of adoration. When we come before the truth of God's very being in Godself, we are often forced to clasp our hands over our mouths so that we do not say too much. It is on our knees in worship that we properly approach an understanding of who God is in Godself. Torrance approvingly quotes

Gregory of Nyssa, who said, "Concepts create idols. Only wonder understands."

———

Finally, it is important to see how Torrance unifies each level of our stratified knowledge of God. We do not leave behind the experience of daily worship and communion with God in the Church when we move to the third level of scientific theology. Instead, we deepen our understanding by more precisely articulating who God is in Godself. These three levels take place from the first to the third, but they are grounded from the third to the first. As God encounters us, as God meets us in our lives through the Holy Spirit and the proclamation of the Gospel, we encounter God's innermost reality and are led to articulate the knowledge of the God who has encountered us.

When we separate the experience of salvation, the evangelical and doxological levels of our knowledge of God, from the truths of God's very being, we can easily fall to the temptation of creating idols. When the theoretical is split from the empirical, our intellectual reasoning from our experience, we wrongfully turn God into a philosophical abstraction. The unification comes from both angles. If we lack either one of these aspects of our knowledge of God, then we will fall into serious errors. Myers makes this point clear in summarizing the value of Torrance's stratification model:

> Finally, perhaps the most valuable aspect of Torrance's model is its emphasis on the continuing correlation between the different levels of theological knowledge. Torrance insists that we must move from the basic level of evangelical experience to the higher levels of scientific conceptualisation without allowing these levels to become detached from one another. On the one hand, our experiential knowledge of Jesus Christ lapses into mere subjectivism if it is detached from its underlying ontological structures; and, on the other hand, our refined theological concepts become meaningless

abstractions if they are severed from the empirical reality of our creaturely world.

— "THE STRATIFICATION OF KNOWLEDGE IN THE
THOUGHT OF T.F. TORRANCE," 13

This model also differentiates between what is essential to Christian theology and what is secondary. It then works as a tool for ecumenical unity, in which we affirm together the essentials without needing to agree fully on secondary issues.

Fundamentally, however, this notion of the stratified levels of knowledge is a helpful implication of *kata physin*. Here Torrance does not develop an abstract theory about how we come to know God but provides a precise model for how we *actually* come to know God through a personal relationship with Jesus Christ in accordance with the nature of God's self-revelation. This is how we come to repentance, to change our minds, and learn to know God in accordance with the truth of His being as Father, Son, and Holy Spirit.

In summary, we must repent from ways of thinking that fail to conform to the reality of God in Christ, and we must remain open to God's reality as God reveals Godself in Christ. These are the two sides of *kata physin*. God reveals Godself first in our experiences of salvation and communion, then as we turn from our experiences to the God whom we experience, we contemplate with awe the innermost being of God as Father, Son, and Holy Spirit. This final level grounds the former levels without leaving them behind. This gives God the primacy over our knowledge of God, making necessary a repentant way of thinking and stressing the openness of our relation to the truth.

SIDEBAR: THE PLACE OF EXPERIENCE IN THEOLOGICAL KNOWLEDGE

Torrance recognizes that our personal experiences with God in salvation, worship, and Church fellowship are essential to a proper theological knowledge of God, though without falling into empty subjectivism. This is a helpful step forward beyond the wrongful divide between those in the Church who pursue so-called "head knowledge" of God (theological) and those who pursue so-called "heart knowledge" of God (experiential).

At the same time, Torrance also avoids abstract objectivism in theological knowledge. Instead of presenting us with a theology of pure theory, one lacking in personal engagement with God, Torrance's theology profoundly integrates our relationship with God in worship and adoration with the theological work of precisely articulating the knowledge of God in the revelation of Jesus Christ.

Torrance's theory of the stratification of knowledge thus negates both pure subjectivism *and* objectivism. This means there is a valid place for our personal experiences with God's love and grace in theological knowledge. Rather than excluding such experiences with God, Torrance includes them as an essential aspect of theology. But, at the same time, these experiences are never without a firm basis in the Word of God, which is why Torrance considers the third level of precise theological knowledge to be the grounding level of all three.

This integration of personal experiences within scientific knowledge explains why Torrance can sometimes make rather staggeringly subjective remarks, such as this one:

> If I may be allowed to speak personally for a moment, I find the presence and being of God bearing upon my experience and thought so powerfully that I cannot but be convinced of his overwhelming reality and rationality. To doubt the existence of God would be an act of sheer irrationality, for it would mean that my reason had become unhinged from its bond with real being.
>
> — THEOLOGICAL SCIENCE, V

If someone were to read this quote without any context or awareness of who T.F. Torrance was, then they may very well conclude that he was a *mystic.* Indeed, there is an element of mystical theology in Torrance's thought, but Torrance was no mystic in the traditional sense of the word (see Myk Habets, *Theology in Transposition,* chapter five). He integrates seamlessly the experiential knowledge of God *within* theological knowledge, but he does not fall back into a purely subjective understanding of God's nature. That is, Torrance does not *base* his theology on pure experience but neither does he discount the fact that experience is *already* integrated into theological thinking. We cannot separate ourselves from our experiences any more than we can jump over our own shadow. We are human beings on this earth who have been brought into a loving relationship with the Triune God, and this has an important role to play in our theological knowledge.

The distinction between those who know God "in their head" and those who know God "in their heart" is nonsense for Torrance. There is no knowledge of God in an impersonal vacuum, neither is there an experience with God's love which is not theologically shaping. This is one of the brilliant implications of the stratification model. Rather than being a theory of pure knowledge or pure experience, Torrance realized we do not know God without first coming into a saving encounter with God by the Holy Spirit. While we must *build* upon these experiences, better articulating the knowledge of God through theological study, this does not *discredit* them or pretend that we will ever leave them behind. We theologically refine the knowledge of the God who has encountered us personally. We do not become theological robots, merely crunching abstract numbers on a machine. We remain human beings, persons who feel and engage in a loving relationship with God in the fellowship of the Church.

In the Church today, we far too often encounter those who scoff at the pursuit of theology as an empty endeavor, as if it were a pursuit leading *away* from a "real" relationship with God. I could not tell you how many times I have met people in the Church who questioned why I love to study theology (especially considering my Charismatic/Methodist upbringing, which tended to emphasize experiences over theology, as if they were mutually exclusive). They would tell me, "I don't need theology, I just love Jesus"—as if to say that loving Jesus excludes theology, or that studying theology excludes loving Jesus. They have fallen prey to a false dualism that separates an experiential knowledge of God from a theological knowledge of God. Yet these individuals ultimately live in a delusion of their own making.

There is no escaping the need for theological knowledge. When people tell me that all they need is to love Jesus and not worry about all that theological stuff, I often think to myself, "Which Jesus is it that you love?" Because, if you want to avoid theological thinking completely, you will end up with an idol named "Jesus" fashioned after your own image. And when that happens, you will be left with what you wanted: a Jesus who makes no demands on your mind, a comfortable little idol to make you feel good about your religiosity. But you won't have the true living God, only an empty reflection of yourself in the mirror.

The real Jesus Christ demands repentance, a *change of mind,* which includes thinking about God in the light of His self-revelation, critically examining our preconceptions, and scientifically apprehending the knowledge of God. Not everyone will study to earn a theology degree, but everyone is called to be a theologian in the Church of Jesus Christ. In fact, every person is a theologian *already,* in one way or another, but those who do not critically examine their thinking likely have a very poor theology indeed. We are called to love God with all our minds (Luke 10:27), and this alone refutes the false distinction between an emotional relation to God and an intellectual one. Both are essential. We must not escape into pure subjectivism with a Jesus of our own making.

But the opposite error is equally possible, and Torrance warns us about it with the same vigor. Professional theologians should not act like abstract mathematicians; God is not an equation to be solved. God is the living God. We fail to speak truthfully when we abstract God's being from God's acts towards us for our salvation in Jesus Christ. If experiential knowledge without objective knowledge ultimately results in subjectivism and the creation of idols, then theoretical knowledge without experience is an empty game without any real grounding in our humanity. We need *both* an evangelical encounter with God and a refined theological knowledge of God.

All of these practical insights are derived from what at first seems like an abstract theory. But, as I hope you now see, Torrance's theory of the stratification of knowledge is far from impractical. Torrance's work opens up the possibility of a theology of Christian experience, which at once remains committed to God's transcendent lordship. Theology is sometimes split between those who pursue a God *without* experience and those who pursue a God named after their experiences (God as a *feeling*). But Torrance opens up an important and practical way beyond both of these limiting perspectives. Think, for example, of the divide between Schleiermacher, the theologian expounding God in the "feeling of absolute dependence," contrasted against Christian fundamentalists, who lock God into a rigid box of pre-established dogmas. Torrance provides space for both the experience of God's love *and* the recognition of God as "Wholly Other" (Barth's term). This returns theology to the *living* God of the scriptures, who was found in the experiences of men and women as their transcendent Lord.

SIDEBAR: APOLOGETICS

After discovering that Torrance's theology engages natural science, many Christians today might wrongly imagine this means Torrance was an *apologist*. The truth, however, is that Torrance was actually quite critical of the task of apologetics, and this is the direct result of his dedication to the concept of *kata physin*.

If true knowledge of God is knowledge in accordance with God's nature, then apologetics is a *false start* because it applies a foreign rationality to God's nature in the attempt to prove that God exists. By taking a foreign rationality and applying it to God, apologetics tries to prove God as if God were not God, as if God were a man or a star in the sky that might be proven through human rationality. Apologetics, therefore, abstracts God into a philosophical construct, which leads me to wonder: even *if* apologetics could "prove" God exists, which God would it prove? It is highly unlikely it would be the Christian God and Father of Jesus Christ, and so what then is the point of proving an empty, abstract deity, who is ultimately just a logical construction of our best thoughts?

Naturally, then, Torrance's primary issue with apologetics is that it contradicts the fundamental axiom of his scientific theology, that true knowledge is knowledge in accordance with the nature of what we seek to know. Apologetics begins with what is rational *to humans,* and not that which is inherent to God's own rationality as revealed in Jesus Christ. Human rationality must be disciplined by God's rationality and not the reverse. God is not the object of human control; we are subject to God's gracious will to reveal Godself. Torrance writes:

> Thus the only kind of evidence for God that will satisfy us is one appropriate to divine nature, appropriate to one who is the ground of His own Being and the Source of all other being, to one whose Being is Spirit and whose nature is love [...] It is this profoundly simple fact, that knowledge of something and the demonstration of its reality must be in accordance with its nature, that lies behind the formation and deployment of the supreme instrument in all scientific knowledge, *the appropriate question.*
>
> — GOD AND RATIONALITY, 53

For Torrance, apologetics is a false enterprise because it relies on asking the wrong kind of questions. It attempts to prove an abstract deity with a rationality alien to the given knowledge of God from the Father, through the Son, and in the Holy Spirit. Where apologetics asks speculatively, "Does God exist?", theology focuses on Jesus Christ as God's self-revelation, as the only true point of contact between God and humanity. Theology asks, "Who is this God revealed in Jesus Christ?" The difference is drastic. There is no logical bridge from humanity up into the knowledge of God, yet God has established, in Jesus Christ, a point of contact through Whom we know God. Thus, it is only by God that we come to know God. Torrance writes:

> I cannot test whether there is a bad smell about by my ear. I cannot verify the presence of a chemical element in some compound by religious experience. Nor can I demonstrate a

proposition in astrophysics by some line of reasoning in aesthetics. All that would obviously be irrational, just as irrational as it would be to put God to the test in some sort of way in which we put nature to the test in carrying through a physical experiment or to demand of Him that He disclose His reality to us through a radar telescope.

— IBID., 93

The core idea behind *kata physin* is the notion that every reality has its own intrinsic rationality to know it by. Apologetics ignores this fact by applying a humanistic, philosophical, or an abstractly logical rationality onto the being of God, thus essentially subjecting God to the provability of human hands. In this sense, Torrance might heartily agree with Bonhoeffer's famous remark, "A God who could be proved by us would be an idol" (*Dietrich Bonhoeffer Works Volume 11,* 260). When we attempt to prove God by a rationality alien to Godself, we ultimately produce a God fashioned after whichever rationality we implement; that is, God becomes an idol. Apologetics is a fundamentally flawed enterprise since it fails to acknowledge God's transcendent *otherness.* Torrance writes:

The transcendent rationality of God, however, is ultimate and as such can be known only out of itself. If God really is God He confronts us with absolute priority. In the nature of the case, He can be known only on the free ground of His own self-subsistent Being and through the shining of His own uncreated Light. The Truth of God cannot be demonstrated from other ground or derive support from lesser truths for He is the ultimate ground and support of them all [...] Knowledge of the ultimate rationality of God is reached at the point where our human reason becomes enlightened from beyond the limits of created rationality and

where an infinite extension of intelligibility beyond ourselves
is disclosed

— GOD AND RATIONALITY, 97

We cannot illuminate God with human insights any more than we
could brighten the moon with a flashlight. The doctrine of justification
by grace alone should lead us to recognize God's provability by grace
alone. Works of the intellect cannot prove God without falling back
into self-justification. God is known when God's uncreated light
reaches us from beyond our humanity, enlightening our rationality
with the divine rationality of God's self-revelation. God alone proves
Godself if God is proven at all, just as God alone reveals Godself if we
have any true knowledge of God's innermost being.

Finally, Torrance writes about the call for repentance as the call for
a new kind of rationality. We are called to embrace God's logic of
God's Self, not a human logic of God reduced down to our own terms.
Repentance implies a turning away from our own rationality to
embrace God's inherent rationality. Thus, Torrance writes:

Michael Polanyi reminds us in his Gifford lectures that we
cannot convince others by formal arguments, for so long as we
argue within their framework, we can never induce them to
abandon it [...] That applies to theological communication as
much as scientific controversy, and yet this is precisely the
erroneous line taken so often by apologetics, whether by the
theologian or the preacher [...] The only proper road to take at
that point is to persuade those operating from the other frame
to look away at the realities we seek to indicate, and to
persuade them to take, in face of it, the kind of 'heuristic'
[personal] step forward which we always have to make in any
genuine scientific discovery, for only then will they discern and
know for themselves what we are speaking about. That is to
say, in theological language, we have to bear witness to the

divine Truth, and try to get from others a genuinely open hearing, but if they take the heuristic [personal] step which they must if they are really to know, it will involve on their part a self-critical act in reconstruction of their prior understanding, i.e., what the New Testament calls *metanoia* [repentance].

— THEOLOGY IN RECONSTRUCTION, 27-8

We should not attempt to make the process *easy* for unbelievers, in the sense that we have to downplay the biblical call to repentance. Instead, Torrance thinks we must give *witness* to the truth of the Gospel without dumbing it down by attempting to remove the inherent *offense* of the good news. Torrance writes:

That is the real difficulty about the Truth of God as it is in Jesus, not a difficulty about language or history in the last resort, but an *offense* which reaches its climax in the Cross [...] The last thing we must ever attempt to do is to eliminate the real difficulties that confront us in the nature of the Truth itself, and so try to make it easy for people to believe and understand—in so doing, we make it next to impossible for them [...] If there were no offense, we would find nothing new in the Scriptures, hear nothing we could not and have not already been able to tell ourselves. That which challenges us, which calls us in question, is the radically new, the element we are unable to assimilate into what we already know, without a logical reconstruction of all our preconceptions and a repentant re-thinking of what we already claim to know. But that is the element in the Scriptures which makes them the means of bringing the Good News—yet in the nature of the case it is Good News, not of some cheap grace that heals the hurts of God's people too lightly, but of radical and complete reconciliation to God through the Cross of Jesus Christ. That

is the only message that really strikes home to the human heart
and meets at last the desperate plight of man.

— IBID., 29

Torrance's scientific axiom that we know in truth only in accordance with what we seek to know (*kata physin*) means the rejection of
apologetics as a false start. His scientific theology does not fit within
the modern Christian "culture war" against science, but it does offer us
a helpful way forward that is faithful to the Gospel and its call for
repentance. Instead of diluting the Gospel with reductionistic logic,
with mere human sensibilities, we must bear witness to God's own
transcendent rationality and call men and women to repent and know
God on God's terms.

3

REFORMULATED NATURAL THEOLOGY

SUMMARY: Torrance agrees with Karl Barth's famous rejection of an *independent* natural theology but goes beyond Barth by integrating (contextualizing) natural theology within divine revelation. This is understood best through the relationship of grace and nature: grace does not *destroy* nature, it perfects and fulfills nature.

IN TORRANCE'S OWN WORDS:

Natural theology cannot be pursued in its traditional abstractive form, as a prior conceptual system on its own, but must be brought within the body of positive theology, and be pursued in indissoluble unity with it. No longer extrinsic but intrinsic to actual knowledge of God, it will function as the necessary intra-structure of theological science, in which we are concerned to unfold and express the rational forms of our understanding that arise under the compulsion of the intelligible reality of God's self-revelation.

— REALITY AND SCIENTIFIC THEOLOGY, 40

A proper natural theology may be pursued only in indissoluble connection with revealed or positive theology, but then it is found to coincide with the epistemological intra-structure of our knowledge of God.

— Ibid., 60

Secondary quotes:

One of Torrance's most significant theological achievements concerns his careful relocation of the place of natural theology within the reformed tradition in general and the Barthian heritage in particular. His understanding of the purpose and place of natural theology has not merely been of major importance in encouraging and fostering the dialogue between Christian theology and the natural sciences; it has also encouraged a new engagement with the doctrine of creation and its implications for this dialogue. One of Torrance's most significant achievements is his redevelopment or redirection of the Barthian critique of natural theology in such a manner that its fundamental principle was retained, while its applicability and utility was enhanced.

— Alister E. McGrath: Participatio, Vol. 1 2009, 73-4

Introduction

In this chapter, we are going to continue examining Torrance's pursuit of a scientific theology by discussing what's been called his "reformulated" or "new" natural theology. This aspect of Torrance's thought will be of particular interest to those familiar with Karl Barth's rejection of natural theology. For Torrance, natural theology is unavoidable. While he rejects any independent forms of natural theology, Torrance does not reject natural theology completely. Instead, Torrance argues for the *integration* or, more precisely, the *contextualization* of natural theology *within* revelation in order to develop ways of thinking that become *natural* to God's self-disclosure. In this chapter, we will look at how Torrance at once agrees with Barth's critique and yet develops it further.

No "INDEPENDENT" NATURAL THEOLOGY

Torrance writes in the preface to the final volume of Barth's *Church Dogmatics*:

> The *Church Dogmatics* has opened up for us the whole perspective of theological understanding in such a way that by standing on Karl Barth's giant shoulders we can see excitingly far into what still needs to be done. It is by going forward into that promise land that we can best show our gratitude for him, and if there we prove for ourselves the immense enlightenment and fruitfulness of his fundamental thought for the further development of Christian theology, we will be able to assess his work and do honour to him in the way he deserves.
>
> — CHURCH DOGMATICS IV/4, VII

Torrance agrees with Barth's rejection of natural theology, yet goes beyond Barth in developing a "reformulated" natural theology. However, there is an important distinction to be made here. Torrance differentiates between any *independent* forms of natural theology from natural theology as an unavoidable reality of human beings, which he then works to *integrate* within divine revelation. We will first look at how Torrance agrees with Barth's rejection of natural theology in its *independent* state.

Traditional natural theology (in Thomas Aquinas, for example) is what Torrance has in mind when he's talking about independent forms of natural theology. Torrance describes this in detail:

[N]atural theology was pursued [classically] as an independent conceptual system, claiming to have its value precisely in that independent status, as a sort of *praeambula fidei* [preamble of faith], antecedent to positive theology, fulfilling a mediating and apologetic function. 'Natural theology' of this kind attempts to reach and teach knowledge of God, apart altogether from any interaction between God and the world, and proceeds by way of abstraction from sense experience and inferential and deductive trains of reasoning beyond observed or empirical facts [...] That is to say, natural theology of this kind represents a desperate attempt to find a *logical bridge* between concepts and experience in order to cross the fatal separation between the world and God which it had posited in its initial assumptions, but it had to collapse along with the notion that science proceeds by way of abstraction from observational data.

— REALITY AND SCIENTIFIC THEOLOGY, 38

For Torrance, this approach is severely problematic, because "by its very operation [natural theology] abstracts the existence of God from his act" (*The Ground and Grammar of Theology,* 89). The God of an independent natural theology ultimately becomes an abstract projection of our best thoughts, since God has been ripped apart from His acts in Jesus. A natural theology developed independently of divine revelation relies on an assumed logical bridge between human concepts and God, but no such bridge can exist. Certainly there is a bridge *from God* to humanity (in the incarnation), but there is no bridge *from humanity* up to the being of God. We cannot take from our world analogies, or even our best rational thoughts, and project them onto God. That's mythology, not proper theological thinking.

Torrance offers a helpful comparison by bringing to mind the relationship of grace and nature in the doctrine of justification. Torrance argues that independent forms of natural theology ultimately ignore the "epistemological implications of justification by grace alone" (ibid., 89-90). That is to say, natural theology rejects God's grace in revelation by attempting to know God by works, by logically lifting itself up into the knowledge of God. None of us would deny that justification is by grace alone (at least I hope we wouldn't). Salvation is an act of God's grace, not the work of any individual. Natural goodness cannot save human beings, no matter how "good" we become. Likewise, since we cannot be justified by works, we also cannot know God through works of the intellect. Knowledge of God, if true, must come from God and not from ourselves, just as salvation, if true, is divinely given through God's abundant grace.

In a clear summary, Torrance writes:

> [J]ustification by Grace alone not only sets aside natural goodness, but sets aside natural theology, for both belong to natural man.
>
> — THEOLOGICAL SCIENCE, 102

Fundamental to the issue of natural theology is how we understand the relationship between grace and nature. Torrance agrees with Barth that God's gracious revelation negates any independent natural theology, but develops beyond him in seeing that grace does not *destroy* nature. Directly following the quotation above, Torrance begins to unveil the core idea behind his reformulated natural theology:

> Just as justification by Grace is not a factual denial of natural goodness, so it is not a metaphysical denial of natural theology, for in neither case is it a denial of natural man in his actual existence, but in both cases it does mean that man is set upon a wholly new basis in Grace. Thus the questioning of natural theology is grounded upon the event of divine grace as relativizing it or excluding it, at least as far as positive approach to God or positive theological inquiry is concerned.
>
> — THEOLOGICAL SCIENCE, 102-3

GRACE DOES NOT DESTROY NATURE

In the same way that justification by grace alone does not deny the existence of natural goodness, so theological justification by grace alone does not deny the existence of natural theology. Natural theology is a fact of our existence as human beings, just as natural goodness is part of who we are. The critical difference, however, is where our ultimate foundation lies. If we rely on natural goodness for salvation, we give into a delusion of self-justification. If we rely on an independent natural theology for true knowledge of God, we likewise delude ourselves with hopeless self-justification. God alone reveals God, and therefore if God is known it is by grace. This does not remove the fact that we remain human beings bound to a natural rationality, a natural knowledge, but it does displace our knowledge as a valid foundation for the knowledge of God. In its place, we find God's knowledge of Godself, shared with us in the mind of Jesus Christ, which becomes the only true foundation for theology. Our rationality still has a part to play, but it is no longer a valid *foundation* for theology to be built upon.

Thus, for Torrance, "Natural theology is not a phenomenon that can simply be brushed aside" (*Transformation & Convergence in the Frame of Knowledge,* 290). Natural theology has its role in a positive theology of revelation, but no longer is it valid for the knowledge of God if it remains independent of revelation. Our natural rationality is not *removed* by revelation, but renewed and reformed—it is made *natural* to divine revelation. "If we are to know God we need to be redeemed from our mental alienation from Him, renewed and reconciled in our minds" (ibid, 291).

Torrance considered this point to be an inconsistency in Barth's rejection of natural theology. Barth failed to consistently implement his own agreement with the fact that nature is not destroyed by grace but is perfected by it. In Barth's theological ethics, he argues this exact idea in other terms. He constructs a brilliant ethic of grace, which does not *destroy* natural goodness but *perfects* it in Christ. Torrance thinks if

Barth would have applied this same understanding of nature and grace consistently with his rejection of natural theology, he would have seen the important role natural theology has to play *in* revealed theology. (Although, Torrance recognized that it is a far more complicated issue than this. In fact, Torrance seemed to think Barth was in essential agreement with him.) Divine revelation does not remove the need for natural theology since revelation cannot remove the human subject who is the recipient of revelation; but revelation reforms and renews our natural theology, forming new modes of thought which arise *naturally* in correspondence to God's self-revelation. God's Word does not make human words about God unnecessary, but it does force a change in human forms of thinking and speaking.

Natural theology should be understood as having an integral part to play together with revelation—not on any *independent* grounds, but by relying upon revelation and thinking in accordance with the truth of God's reality. Torrance writes:

> Natural theology can no longer be pursued in its old abstractive form, as a prior conceptual system on its own, but must be brought within the body of positive theology and be pursued in indissoluble unity with it. But then its whole character changes, for pursued within actual knowledge of the living God where we must think rigorously in accordance with the nature of the divine object, it will be made *natural* to the fundamental subject-matter of theology and will fall under the determination of its inherent intelligibility. No longer extrinsic but intrinsic to actual knowledge of God, it will function as the essential sub-structure within theological science, in which we are concerned to develop the inner material logic that arises in our inquiry and understanding of God.
>
> — Ibid., 295

God's revelation reaches us *as we are,* in our limited creaturely rationality. To set aside natural theology would be to obliterate human beings and our natural ways of thinking. Our rationality is *transformed* by revelation; it is not altogether set aside.

AN EXAMPLE FROM GEOMETRY AND PHYSICS

Torrance uses an analogy to help explain his point. Euclidean geometry was classically a subject studied in isolation from the physical realities it seeks to describe. Think back to math class, when you were taught to calculate two-dimensional shapes on a piece of paper. These abstract forms lack any concrete basis in reality. In order to become relevant for physics, two-dimensional geometry was forced to be *integrated* and *transformed* in our multi-dimensional world. This is similar to what happens with natural theology when it is integrated within revelation. Torrance explains this at length:

> All this must not be taken to mean the end of natural theology, however, but rather its need for a radical reconstruction through a profounder way of coordinating our thought with being. What is involved here may be indicated by drawing an analogy taken from modern physics and the problem it has had to face in coordinating geometrical concepts and experience and which it came to solve by taking its cue from Riemannian geometry of space-time. Euclidean geometry is pursued and developed *a priori* [theoretically], as an independent science on its own, antecedent to physics, but is then found to be finally irrelevant to the actual structure of the universe of space and time. Everything changes, however, when geometry is introduced into the material content of physics as a four dimensional physical geometry, for then it becomes what Einstein called 'a natural science' in indissoluble unity with physics. So it is with natural theology: brought within the embrace of positive theology and developed as a complex of rational structures arising in our actual knowledge of God it becomes 'natural' in a new way, natural to its proper object, God in self-revealing interaction with us in space and time. Natural theology then constitutes the epistemological

'geometry', as it were, within the fabric of 'revealed theology' as it is apprehended and articulated within the objectivities and intelligibilities of the space-time medium through which God has made himself known to us. As such, however, natural theology has no independent status but is the pliant conceptual instrument which Christian theology uses in unfolding and expressing the content of real knowledge of God through modes of human thought and speech that are made rigorously appropriate to his self-revelation to mankind.

— REALITY AND SCIENTIFIC THEOLOGY, 39

Torrance is concerned here with the unity of *form* and *being*. Natural theology operates as a "necessary *intra-structure* of theological science" (ibid., 40). Natural theology provides a necessary *form* for the knowledge which corresponds to the *being* of God we come to know in revelation.

If you shoot an arrow up into the sky, it will inevitably fall back down on your head. If you form a natural theology *independent* of God's actual self-revelation, you'll ultimately land back on yourself with a kind of theological anthropomorphism. However, when natural theology is integrated within God's self-revelation, it forms the necessary intra-structure of our knowledge of God. Therefore, natural theology is *necessary* but not *sufficient*.

Torrance was fond of using another analogy to help understand the way natural theology must conform to the content of revelation, which he borrowed from Michael Polanyi. The analogy is essentially this: imagine you are forced to wear a pair of glasses that invert your vision. Everything is reversed: right is left, left is right, up is down, and down is up. The problem now becomes how to adjust to this new form of reality. Undoubtedly, at first you will struggle, stumbling around helplessly, but over time you will adjust by forming a new intuitive understanding of the world. Your rationality will eventually conform to the new reality forced on your mind by these inverted spectacles.

Likewise, natural theology must be transformed into the new environment forced upon it by God's self-revelation. Our natural knowledge is called into question by revelation. We must *repent* of our false rationality and learn to have our rationality *transformed* by God's Word. Just as inverted spectacles would force a radical adjustment in how our minds relate to the world, so natural theology, our structures and ways of thinking about God, must radically be disciplined and conform to the actual knowledge of God in Jesus Christ. We must learn to think consistently with God's self-revelation. Revelation cannot fit within *our* modes of thought but must be *transformed* to rightly correspond to God's Word. This is what Torrance is concerned about in his reformulated natural theology.

Here we can see that Torrance's work on natural theology follows his central conviction of *kata physin* (knowledge according to nature). This is, of course, not knowledge according to *our* nature but according to God's. We have a natural theology, a natural rationality, each one of us, but if we are to know God in a way appropriate to God's nature, our natural theologies are required to be contextualized within divine revelation. This is Torrance's point.

It is worth noting that Torrance may have regretted using the term "natural theology" to express this idea since it tends to confuse the matter more than help. (See Colyer, *How to Read T.F. Torrance*, 194 n. 187.) We could perhaps be more faithful to Torrance's intent if we speak of contextualizing our natural *rationality*, or our natural forms of thought, by revelation, instead of bringing in the term "natural theology" with all its historical baggage. Torrance still fits within Barth's adamant refusal to place any value on natural revelation, but using the term "natural theology" makes it appear as if Torrance stands in complete disagreement with Barth. Torrance actually thinks Barth's teaching is quite close to his own on this issue, though not identical. (See Torrance's preface to *Space, Time and Resurrection*, x.) However, since Torrance's work consistently uses the term "natural theology," I have retained that same usage here.

4

ONE IN BEING AND ACT (HOMOOUSION)

SUMMARY: The being and acts of the Father and the Son are *one* and not divided (*homoousion*: "one in being"). This is a central doctrine in Torrance's theology. The truth of the Gospel depends on the *homoousion*, on the unity of the Son with the Father. For us practically, this doctrine reveals that there is no God behind the back of Jesus Christ for us to fear. The life and work of Jesus Christ are intrinsic to the very being of God; in Him, it is truly God's being and acts as a human.

IN TORRANCE'S OWN WORDS:

If there is no unbreakable bond of being between Jesus Christ and God, then we are left with a dark inscrutable Deity behind the back of Jesus Christ of whom we can only be terrified. If there is no relation of mutual knowing and being and loving between the incarnate Son and the Father, then Jesus Christ does not go bail, as it were, for God, nor does he provide for us any guarantee in what he was or said or did as to what God is like in himself.

— The Mediation of Christ, 59

Everything depends upon the unity in being and act and word between Jesus Christ the only begotten Son and God the Father. If the [oneness in being with the Father] were not true, the Gospel would lack the very foundation in the self-revelation or self-communication of God in Jesus Christ which it needs in order to be Gospel [...] The *homoousion* asserts that God *is* eternally in himself what he *is* in Jesus Christ, and, therefore, that there is no dark unknown God behind the back of Jesus Christ, but only he who is made known to us in Jesus Christ.

— The Trinitarian Faith, 135

Secondary quotes:

[F]or Torrance it is only because God has revealed himself to us through Christ and in the Spirit that we can speak about God [...] Here the *homoousion* is utterly decisive and revolutionary in Torrance's mind, for it expresses the supreme evangelical truth of the Gospel that God is the content of what God is towards us in God's love and grace, what God has done and continues to do for us in Jesus Christ and the Holy Spirit, God really is in Himself.

— Elmer E. Colyer: How to Read T.F. Torrance, 151

Introduction

Homoousion is a precise theological term, borrowed from Greek, which refers to the oneness in being and act of the Father and the Son. Torrance often calls this doctrine the "linchpin" of the Gospel; without it, the whole Christian faith falls to pieces. He even goes on to say, "The most outstanding feature of the Gospels is their presentation of the oneness of Jesus and his Father" (*A Passion for Christ*, 9). This chapter provides an overview and history of the *homoousion,* as well as a discussion of its importance for Torrance's theology.

The history and usage of the *Homoousion*

Following the first council of Nicaea in 325, the doctrine of the *homoousion* was formally agreed upon as an essential confession for the Christian faith. The ecumenical council met primarily regarding the Arian controversy. Arius had subordinated the divinity of the Son to the Father, thereby arguing that the Son was merely the firstborn of creation, instead of eternal with the Father. In opposition to Arius, the council agreed upon a document which today is often considered to be the epitome of orthodox theology: the Nicene Creed.

The heretic Arius argued for the doctrine of *homoiousian,* denoting a "similarity" of being shared by the Father and the Son. The Patristic fathers adamantly rejected this notion, since it subordinates, and ultimately undermines, Christ's divinity. Instead, they agreed upon the *homoousion,* the *oneness* in being/substance of the Father and the Son. This decision established the *homoousion* as a quintessential confession for Trinitarian theology and Christian orthodoxy. The Nicene Creed, repeated still today, confesses: "[We believe] in one Lord Jesus Christ, the Son of God [...] Light of Light, very God of very God, begotten not made, being of one substance with the Father [*homoousion to Patri*]."

This final phrase is simple enough, but an insistence upon the *homoousion to Patri,* according to Torrance, is essential for the whole Christian faith. There is no Gospel without it. Torrance writes on the significance of this decision:

The basic decision taken at Nicaea made it clear that the eternal relation between the Father and the Son in the Godhead was regarded in the Church as the supreme truth upon which everything else in the Gospel depends. Jesus Christ is himself the content of God's unique self-revelation to mankind. It is on the ground of what God has actually revealed of his own nature in him as his only begotten Son that everything else to be known of God and of his relation to the world and human beings is to be understood. It is only when we know God the Father in and through his Son who belongs to his own being as God that we may know him in any true and accurate way, that is, know God strictly in accordance with his divine nature. In order to know him in that way, however, we must enter into an intimate and saving relationship with him in Jesus Christ his incarnate Son, for it is only through reconciliation to God by the blood of Christ that we may draw near to him and have access to him […] Thus the very essence of the Gospel and the whole of the Christian Faith depends on the centrality and primacy of the relation in being and agency between Jesus Christ and God the Father.

— THE TRINITARIAN FAITH, 3

The *homoousion* is a precise theological term, like the "Trinity," which expresses a reality that can be only *indicated* by human speech, though it is at once beyond human comprehension. Since the *homoousion* is a theological term used with a particular purpose in mind, it will be helpful to recognize the way Torrance uses precise terminology such as this. Torrance writes like a scientist, using words and phrases with care. We saw this with his definition of a proper science, as well as his adoption of the Greek phrase *kata physin*. In the same way, Torrance's usage of the *homoousion* is technical. Torrance has many insightful things to say about statements of truth and their relation to the truth of their statements. In this context, he writes:

There is a measure of impropriety in all human language of God, and therefore [we] must ever be ready to call a halt in speaking of him, in humble acknowledgement of the fact that our human thought cannot travel beyond a certain point, and be ready at the same time to let the human speech used by the Holy Spirit in the Scriptures point far beyond itself to the sheer reality and glory of God who alone can bear witness of himself and create in us, beyond any capacity of our own to achieve it, genuine knowledge of God [...] The primary reference of theological statements is to the Reality of God infinitely beyond and above us [...].

— THEOLOGY IN RECONSTRUCTION, 31

Statements of truth do not contain truth in themselves but point away from themselves to the truth that they indicate. If I say, "The house is blue," this is obviously true only if the house is actually blue. The statement itself is inadequate if it does not point *beyond* itself to a truth in reality. If the house were not blue, my statement would be nonsense. Statements of truth are dependent upon the truth of their statements. In a similar way, it is important to note that the doctrine of the *homoousion,* alongside other theological terms, is not a self-grounded statement, as if it exists independent of the reality it indicates, but it is grounded in the transcendent reality of God. The *homoousion* indicates a mystery at the heart of the Gospel: God in Christ, the incarnation of the Son of God as a human being.

The Nicene usage of the *homoousion to Patri* has chief importance not only for Torrance's theology but for the whole Christian Church. This was not constructed in isolation from reality but was forced upon the mind of the Patristic Fathers as they thought through the truth of God and the incarnation. This is important to clarify for those who might condemn the *homoousion* as "extra-biblical." The same could be said for other essential theological terms such as the "Trinity" or the "hypostatic union" (neither of which appear in the Bible).

The importance of the *homoousion* cannot be quickly brushed aside; it is essential for the Gospel. We will now consider the reasons why Torrance stresses a return to the centrality of this doctrine. It is not because the statement itself is important apart from the reality it indicates, but that through the *homoousion* we are led to contemplate the profound mystery of Jesus Christ, who is one in being and act with the Father in the Holy Spirit. It is with awe and humility that we dare speak of God's innermost being.

No God but the God revealed in Jesus

The *homoousion* means: "[T]here is no God except the God who has come and meets us in Jesus" (*A Passion for Christ*, 13). Who God is and what God is like can be known in Jesus Christ and not elsewhere. Torrance often remarked, "There is no unknown God behind the back of Jesus Christ for us to fear" (ibid., 55). When we fear that perhaps God is *not* like Jesus, we are failing to consider the significance of the *homoousion*. This doctrine solidifies our knowledge of the God revealed in Christ.

One of the most disturbing tendencies of Western theology is an unspoken, but often implied, divide between the being and acts of God and the being and acts of Jesus Christ. Few will outright deny the *homoousion*, but in our talk of God, we often deny it in practice by isolating Christ from His Father. We deny the incarnation and God's self-revealing when we seek after a knowledge of God that does not rely wholly upon the person and work of Jesus Christ, which does not see in Him the inseparable bond of the Father, Son, and Holy Spirit.

What if we refused to determine our doctrine of God by any philosophy, any theology, or even any scripture verse removed from its proper context, and instead, what if our doctrine of God was adamantly shaped and controlled by the incarnate life and passion of the Son of God? This would result in nothing less than a revolution in the doctrine of God. All those foreign ideas of a hidden will in God would be undone, and all the philosophical constructs of what God "must" be like if God is to be God would shatter. In Jesus Christ, we see the face of God, and there is no God except for the God found in Him. The *homoousion* insists we take Jesus Christ seriously as the center and source of all true knowledge of God.

Most believers today will confess a profound trust in Jesus Christ; but when you ask these same believers what they think about Jesus' *Father,* their answers are often astounding. The way we talk about the Father of Jesus Christ as an angry, irritable, grace-less God, hidden somewhere behind the back of Jesus, is a disgrace to the *homoousion.* The Gospel falls to pieces without a firm awareness that *this is what God is like,* God is like Jesus. No other factor should determine our knowledge of God more than Jesus Christ; no theoretical ideas about God should be given more weight than the self-revelation of God in Him.

The importance of the *homoousion,* then, is twofold. First, it is essential for securing the knowledge of God. If God's being is not one and the same between the Father and the Son, then there is no assurance we have any knowledge of God at all. Only God can reveal God, and if Christ does not share in the being of God, then He cannot truly reveal God to us. We would be thrown back upon ourselves, resigned to our vain mythological speculations. However, if the oneness in being and act of the Father and the Son remains a firm conviction in our minds, then we have certainty that it is *God* who has truly reached us and made God's being known. The fearful tendency to imagine God as a lightning bolt in the sky, as a kind of Zeus-like deity, is a failure to take seriously the implications of the *homoousion.*

Second, the *homoousion* means it was truly God who acted for us and with us in Jesus Christ. It was not a human, not even the best of humanity, who saved us, but truly God as a human being, God in the thick of our darkness and estrangement, who lifts us up into the Triune communion of God's light and love. Salvation must be *of* God or else it is not truly a salvation which restores us *to* God. In this sense, the oneness in being and act of the Son and the Father establishes the reality of our salvation, reconciliation, and redemption in Him. If it is not truly God who reaches us in the incarnate life of Jesus Christ, then we are not reconciled to God at all.

Perhaps in this light, it becomes easier to see why Torrance calls this doctrine the linchpin of the Gospel. Without a firm conviction of the truth of the *homoousion* there is no reality of salvation, no certainty in our knowledge of God, and no assurance that we are loved and cherished by Him. In short, there is no good news at all; we would remain lost in our darkness and sin, lost in a fearful, alienated state of existence. The *homoousion* is essential to the truth of the Gospel.

Torrance writes on the damage caused by neglecting the *homoousion*:

> Any such detachment or disjunction between the being and nature of Jesus and the being and nature of God could only disrupt the message of grace and peace which the Gospel brings, and it would introduce the deepest anxiety into human life born of the dreadful fear that God may turn out in the end to be utterly different from what we see in Jesus Christ, fear lest there is behind the back of Jesus some dark inscrutable God, some arbitrary Deity of whom we can know nothing but before whom in our guilty conscience as sinners we cannot but quake and shiver in our souls.
>
> — A PASSION FOR CHRIST, 16

But when we take seriously the *homoousion,* we are baptized in a firm assurance of the goodness and love of God towards us, as Torrance writes definitively:

> [In the Gospels] he who had seen Jesus had seen the Father, so that there was no ground for anxiety or fear. What the Father is and does, Jesus is and does. And what Jesus is and does, the Father is and does.

There is in fact no God behind the back of Jesus, no act of God other than the act of Jesus, no God but the God we see and meet in him. Jesus Christ is the open heart of God, the very love and life of God poured out to redeem humankind, the mighty hand and power of God stretched out to heal and save sinners.

— IBID., 17

As we can see it is imperative to keep central the *homoousion* of the Father, Son, and Holy Spirit. This is because only God can reveal Godself, and only God can save humanity. If at any moment during the incarnate life of the Son, the Father is detached or incongruent with the being and act of the Son, then the bottom falls out of the Gospel and everything becomes irrational. This is what is at stake, and this is why Torrance stresses a return to the centrality of the *homoousion* so forcefully throughout his work.

Dualism

We've already discussed Torrance's critique of dualism in chapter one, but now that we have considered the *homoousion* we can see the full perspective of why Torrance rejects dualism. One of the most problematic dualisms affecting Christian thought today is the dualism between the Father and the Son. Torrance's emphasis on the *homoousion* makes it impossible to retain this sort of thinking. We cannot contemplate the Father as an idea far removed from Jesus' historical existence, or as a separate being somewhere else entirely. The Gospel only makes sense in the unity of Their life together. Any understanding of Jesus that does not reveal the "Abba" He loved collapses Christ into a moral example we must imitate, instead of the gracious Son who has reconciled the world to the Father by the Holy Spirit.

Giving mere lip service to the doctrine of the *homoousion* will not overcome the (mostly) unspoken notion of a divided Father and Son. We need a firmer grasp on the oneness in being and act of the Father, the Son, and the Holy Spirit if we are to overcome the dualistic thought which has reeked havoc on the doctrine of God. Torrance's theology is a shining example of a way forward beyond this dualism, and we should follow his lead by returning to an emphasis on the *homoousion*.

SIDEBAR: TRIUNE AT-ONE-MENT

A natural test case for the *homoousion* is an examination of the Son's "God-forsaken" death on the cross, particularly the horrific cry, "My God, my God, why have you forsaken me?" It is my opinion that the Church today fails to adequately take the *homoousion* seriously most of all in its doctrine of the atonement. Torrance offers a holistic view of the atonement by refusing to split apart the oneness in being and act of the Father, Son, and Holy Spirit—*especially* in the Son's cry of abandonment from the cross.

How does Torrance relate the importance he gives to the *homoousion* with this cry? Torrance writes, with reference to Gregory of Nazianzen:

> What about the passion and sacrifice of Christ in which, as our Lord claimed, he gave himself for the redemption of mankind? What would be the message of the Cross if Christ and God were ultimately divided there, Christ only a creature on earth, and God infinitely removed in the exaltation of his divine being? How could the great reconciling exchange have taken place unless it was God himself who in his infinite loving-

kindness had come in Jesus Christ to make our nature, our sin and our death his own, in order to save us? [...] Only if God himself were directly and immediately engaged in the passion of Christ could it be the vicarious means of redeeming and liberating the creation. 'God crucified'! That is what Gregory of Nazianzen in an Easter oration once declaimed as a 'miracle'. 'We needed an incarnate God, a God put to death, that we might live. We were put to death together with him, that we might be cleansed; we rose again with him, because we were put to death with him; we were glorified with him, because we rose again with him.' [*Orations,* 45.28f] Atoning reconciliation would be utterly empty of content, had not God the incarnate Son, true God from true God, suffered and died for us on the Cross.

— THE TRINITARIAN FAITH, 142

It is essential we see it was truly *God* who suffered for our sakes on the cross, that the Son, the Father, and the Holy Spirit were in one accord, that their oneness in being and agency was not cut. We must see the *homoousion* clearly, even at the darkest moment of human history, because if the oneness of the being and act of God fails here, it fails everywhere.

The commonly held notion that the Father forsook the Son, abandoning Him to death and turning His back on Him, is a result of failing to take the *homoousion* seriously. To better understand this, let us first consider what Torrance wrote in this quotation:

If the Lord Jesus Christ is, as the Nicene Creed expressed it, the only-begotten Son of the Father, begotten from his Father before all ages, true God of true God, then the Father/Son or Son/Father relation falls within the eternal being of God, the Sonship of God being just as eternal in God as the Fatherhood of God, for God the Father is not Father apart from the Son, and God the Son is not Son apart from the Father. The revelation of God in the saving acts of Jesus Christ as Father and Son is grounded in and issues from the inner being of the one eternal God [...] what God is toward us in the revealing and saving acts of Jesus Christ he is in eternally and immanently in himself, and what God is in himself eternally and immanently in himself as Father and Son he actually is toward us in the revealing and saving acts of Jesus Christ.

— THE MEDIATION OF CHRIST, 111-2

If it truly was the Son of God who suffered and died on the cross, then the work of atonement falls within the inner life of the Holy Trinity. This was not an event *external* to God's being but truly inherent to the life of God. This is why Torrance writes on the same page, "The cross is a window opened into the very heart of God" (ibid.). Because the oneness in being and act of the Father, Son, and Holy Spirit is an essential element of what makes God *God,* then the atonement must be understood as taking place *within* this unity and not apart from it. Any notion of an internal division between God and God on the cross fails to understand the implications of the *homoousion* for the atonement.

The oneness in being of the Father and the Son is often called into question exactly where it should be made known the most forcefully: in the doctrine of the atonement. Far too often we speak about the atonement as a kind of external *transaction* that took place between God and Jesus Christ. We then wonder why so many Christians ask, "Is God *really* like Jesus?" We have split apart the seamless acts of the Father and the Son, and it should not then surprise us when believers question their continuity.

While Torrance may not say as much himself, I think one central reason why Christians today doubt that God is really like Jesus can be traced back to failing to recognize the *homoousion* in the atonement. I can personally attest to this. I was taught in my Sunday school classes that on the cross God the Father, in anger and disgust, turned His back on the Son He loves. Reading Torrance was like a breath of fresh air for me. His insistence on the oneness in being and act of God, *especially in the atoning death of Jesus Christ,* radically changed my perception of God. I no longer operate with a dualistic way of thinking about God, in which Jesus is somehow different from His Father; my understanding of the cross no longer *leads* me to assume any sort of division. The notion that the Father indifferently forsook the Son, coldly abandoning Him to suffer and die, is one of the most damaging ideas in the Church today, because it calls into question the oneness in being and act of the Son with the Father, thereby driving a wedge between Jesus Christ and God.

What we need is a healthy understanding of the *pain* of the Father who also suffered by giving up His dearly beloved Son. God the Father was not unaffected by the events of Calvary but deeply and personally *in pain* over the death of the Son—though rightly we must say it was the Son alone who died (this is not a pass at patripassianism). The same should be said of the Holy Spirit, who was not without *grief* over the Son's death. The *homoousion* means that the crucifixion of Jesus Christ was an event *in the life of God,* not a legal fiction which took place outside of God's Triune being. Accordingly, Torrance writes:

> The fact that the Father did not spare his only Son but delivered him up for us all, as St Paul expressed it, tells us that in the sacrifice of Christ on the cross it was the Father as well as the Son who paid the cost of our salvation, so that through the blood of Christ the innermost nature of God the Father as holy love became revealed to us [...] Thus the atonement is to be regarded as the act of God in his being and his being in his act.
>
> — THE MEDIATION OF CHRIST, 112-3

ABANDONED OR DEPENDENT?

If all this is true—if the atonement is an event in the life of God—then what do we say about the Son's horrible cry of abandonment, "My God, my God, why have you forsaken me?" Was the Son *actually* abandoned by the Father?

It is important to remember that Jesus was quoting Psalm twenty-two. In the context of that Psalm, it will be helpful to distinguish between what was *actually* happening and what the Psalmist *felt* in that moment. Like many of the Psalms, there is a change in tone from beginning to end. Oftentimes, the feeling of the Psalmist is more essential to understanding the Psalm than any literal event taking place. Think, for example, of Psalm twenty-three. Is the Psalmist actually walking through a valley, or literally sitting down to a table with the Lord in the presence of their enemies? None of us focus on mere literal events in the Psalms, but why do we then treat Jesus' cry so literally?

Psalm twenty-two begins in despair over God's supposed absence, but it ends with a triumphant realization that God had never left the Psalmist's side. This is a profound clarification of what was actually taking place in the life of the Psalmist, against what they were feeling at the time. We read this realization in verse twenty-four: "For he *did not* despise or abhor the affliction of the afflicted; *he did not hide his face from me*, but heard when I cried to him" (emphasis mine). God did not forsake the Psalmist, even though the Psalmist very much *felt* abandoned by God. Likewise, Jesus' usage of this Psalm has to reckon with its whole context and purpose. It was not that the Father had *actually* forsaken the Son, but that the Son *felt* forsaken by taking up *our* experiences of abandonment as His own. Understanding this Psalm in its context sheds significant light on Christ's cry of abandonment.

In Jewish culture, Psalm twenty-two would have been very well known—and not as an isolated quotation, but in its entirety from beginning to end. It would be like singing the first line of a popular song everyone knows from the radio. The whole song is brought to mind with its beginning. Those present at the crucifixion would have likely recalled not just a single line from the Psalm but the major theme of the Psalm, which is the recognition of God's solidarity with us even in our darkness and despair. It means that even when it feels like God has abandoned us, God is always near and has not turned away. We should keep in mind the fact that Jesus' cry cannot be merely an isolated statement, but it is best understood within the context of the whole Psalm, which emphasized God's solidarity with us in the midst of our darkness.

Torrance argues that Jesus' cry on the cross was *our* cry, which He took up as His own, while at once refuting it. This is illustrated well by Jesus' second cry, His cry of sonship, "Father, into your hands I commend my spirit." Notice the essential difference in how Jesus prays from one to the other. The cry of abandonment was prayed before an unknown "god," while the cry of dependence addressed God as "Father," as Jesus' dear Abba.

In Jesus' cry of abandonment, He took up, as His own, *our* suffering cries before a silent, distant, unknown "god." But Jesus never addressed His Father as "god." Jesus' Father is His dear "Abba," not some unknown deity. The difference between these two prayers should make it abundantly clear what was really taking place. The cry of trust, "Father, into your hands I commend my spirit," is a prayer Jesus would actually pray. The cry of abandonment was not Jesus' prayer, but *our prayer,* the prayer of a fallen humanity that fears God. Christ joined us in the thick of our suffering, and He entered our experiences of abandonment on the cross. The second cry, however, is the *conversion* of our cries of hopelessness to share in His declaration of unwavering trust. Jesus had taken up our fallen human mind that perceives God's absence, and He converted it to know God rightly as His dear Abba.

Jesus told the disciples quite plainly what would happen on the cross: "A time is coming and in fact has come when you will be scattered to your own home. You will leave me all alone. Yet I am not alone, for my Father is with me" (John 16:32). He knew even then that His Father would never abandon Him. Jesus' unwavering trust in His Father, lived out from within our fallen humanity, means the conversion of our fallen cries of abandonment into a loving declaration of trust. He took up *our* prayers of hopelessness and converted them into His prayer of dependence. Torrance summarizes all this well:

'My God, my God, why hast thou forsaken me?' That was a cry of utter God-forsakenness, *the despairing cry of man in his dereliction which Jesus had made his own*, taking it over from the twenty-second Psalm, thereby revealing that he had penetrated into the ultimate horror of great darkness, the abysmal chasm that separates sinful man from God. But there in the depths where we are exposed to the final judgements of God, *Jesus converted man's atheistical shout of abandonment and desolation into a prayer of commitment and trust*, 'Father into thy hands I commend my spirit.' *The Son and the Father were one and not divided*, each dwelling in the other, even in that 'hour and power of darkness' when Jesus was smitten of God and himself descended to the very bottom of our human existence where we are alienated and antagonistic, into the very hell of our godlessness and despair, laying fast hold of us and taking our cursed condition upon himself, in order to embrace us for ever in his reconciling love.

— THE MEDIATION OF CHRIST, 43; EMPHASIS MINE.

Furthermore, Torrance recognizes that the resurrection reaffirmed God's unbroken fellowship on the cross:

The resurrection means that this union did not give way but held under the strain imposed not only by the forces that sought to divide Jesus from God, but the strain imposed through the infliction of the righteous judgement of the Father upon our rebellious humanity which Christ made his own—

and it held under the strain imposed by both in the crucifixion: the hypostatic union survived the descent into hell and Christ arose still in unbroken communion with the Father. The resurrection is thus the resurrection of the union forged between man and God in Jesus out of the damned and lost condition of men into which Christ entered in order to share their lot and redeem them from doom.

— Space, Time and Resurrection, 54

There is no dark, hidden God to fear behind the back of Jesus Christ; there is only the God who has made Godself known in Him. Even on the cross, the Father and the Son were in one accord and not divided. To imply such a notion would be to destroy the very heart of the Gospel, as well as the *at-one-ment* of the cross. By applying the *homoousion* to the event of Christ's crucifixion, Torrance has helped clarify the unity of God in atonement and removed any need to fear a God behind the back of Jesus Christ. The being and act of the Father and the Son remained united in indestructible oneness—especially on the cross.

SIDEBAR: ELECTION

Karl Barth is well known for his radical revision to the Reformed doctrine of election (see *Church Dogmatics* II/2). Torrance discusses the doctrine less than his teacher did, but his work on election shares many of the same convictions as Barth's doctrine. We will not explore every aspect and difficulty of the doctrine here. Instead, I will assume you have a basic understanding of Barth's doctrine of election and only point out some of the ways Torrance agrees and develops upon Barth's doctrine. If you are unfamiliar with Barth's work on election, see my former book, *Karl Barth in Plain English,* chapter five.

Torrance applies the *homoousion* to the doctrine of election, which results in a non-speculative election centered on the person of Jesus Christ. Torrance writes:

> There is for us no activity of God behind the back of Jesus Christ or apart from the mission of the Spirit, for there is only one movement of God's Love, one movement of his

Grace, and one movement of divine Sanctification, which freely flows to us from the Father through the Son and in the Holy Spirit, which took concrete form in our human existence in space and time in the incarnate economy of redemption.

— THE CHRISTIAN DOCTRINE OF GOD, 108

We cannot think of election specifically, or of God's eternal purposes for humanity generally, apart from the concrete history of Jesus Christ. This is what we learn from the *homoousion*. Therefore, election is centered not around an abstract decree, but concretely election *is* Jesus Christ. Torrance writes:

Election is the person of Christ, true God and true man in one person, the union of the Father and the Son in eternal love incarnated in our flesh, and bodied forth among sinners. And so men and women in history, in their temporal actions and relations, in the midst of their temporal choices and decisions, are confronted by the Word made flesh, with the eternal decision of God's eternal love. In Jesus Christ, therefore, eternal election has become *temporal event.*

— INCARNATION, 180

Since, "Election rests on the relation of love between the Father and the Son" (ibid., 178) and operates within God's Triune life of love, then "Jesus Christ is identical with God's decision and man's election in the divine love" (ibid.). And as such:

Election means, therefore, that Christ assumes our flesh, assumes our fallen estate, assumes our judgment, assumes our reprobation, in order that we may participate in his glory, and share in the union of the Son with the Father.

— IBID.

Like Barth, Torrance thinks the weakness of Calvin's doctrine of election was a far too general concept of God's acts rather than a specific focus on the history of the person of Jesus Christ. This is why Torrance insists that Jesus Christ is not only the true elect of God but, in assuming our flesh, He has also assumed *our reprobation.* He is, then, the one true elect man for our sakes *and* the one true reprobate in our place. While Calvin, we might argue, sought after an abstract eternal decree hidden behind Jesus Christ, Torrance is interested in the concrete eternal decree that has become a temporal event in Him. Thus, Torrance writes:

> Whatever we do, we cannot speak of an election or a predestination behind the back of Jesus Christ, and so divide God's saving action in two, into election and into the work of Christ on the cross. God's eternal election is nothing else than God's eternal love incarnate in his beloved Son, so that in him we have election incarnate. God's eternal decree is nothing other than God's eternal Word so that in Christ we have the eternal decree or Word of God made flesh. Election is identical with the life and existence and work of Jesus Christ, and *what he does is election going into action.*

— ATONEMENT, 183

Torrance stands close to Barth in his understanding of the election of Jesus Christ, but Torrance has also made a few notable clarifications. This includes the emphasis on God's eternal election becoming flesh in Christ and the assumption of our humanity including the assumption of our reprobation. We don't have time to work out further these clarifications or explore all the details of how Torrance's doctrine of election fits within his theology, but it is still important to note where Torrance stands.

Briefly stated, election is the love of the Father towards the Son in the Holy Spirit, the eternal decree of God's being, turned outwards towards us and made incarnate in our humanity. In the election of Jesus Christ, human beings are elected to be the children of God. Jesus is the one elect man in whom all find themselves elected by freely and personally participating in His election, that is, in His relationship with the Father. It was Their relationship that became incarnate, as the Son maintained communion with the Father and the Spirit during the entirety of His life and ministry as a human. God's love and free decision to be our God (election) became incarnate in the Word made flesh.

This also includes the fact that Jesus Christ is the one and only *reprobate* human in our place, and upon Him the judgment of God was suffered as the sinner is set free from sin and guilt. Torrance discusses the doctrine of election in only a few of his works, but it is most consistently discussed in relation to the atonement. He has in mind the "divine exchange," in which God, as a human, takes up our cause, suffers our death, and raises us up from the dead together with Him to share in the Triune life of God.

Rather than an abstract God and an arbitrary selection of human beings, Torrance refocuses the doctrine back upon the person of Jesus Christ as both the electing God and elected human. There is no election behind the back of Jesus Christ, just as there is no God who remains hidden behind Him. Only as we look to Jesus do we come to understand eternal election in our humanity.

This doctrine fits within the context of the *homoousion,* because, for Torrance, the *homoousion* radically reorients our understanding of God's being and acts. Election considered apart from Jesus is empty and abstract speculation. The *homoousion* puts an end to any doctrine of election constructed independently of Jesus Christ.

Thus, Torrance summarizes the doctrine:

Election means nothing more and nothing less than the complete action of God's eternal love, that "God so loved the world that He gave His only begotten Son that whosoever believeth on Him should not perish but have everlasting life." [John 3:16, KJV] It is the eternal decision of God who will not be without us entering time as grace, choosing us and appropriating us for Himself, and who will not let us go. Election is the love of God enacted and inserted into history in the life, death, and resurrection of Jesus Christ, so that in the strictest sense Jesus Christ is the election of God. He is the one and indivisible act of divine love. There is therefore no decree of predestination which precedes this act of grace or goes behind the back of Jesus Christ, for that would be to split the act of God into two, and to divide Christ from God. Jesus Christ is wholly identical with God's action, that which was, and that which is, and that which shall be, the same yesterday, to-day, and forever.

— "UNIVERSALISM OR ELECTION?", 314-5

DETERMINISM AND THE SCIENTIFIC OUTLOOK

One of the fascinating aspects of Torrance's work on election is how it compliments so well his dialogue with the natural sciences. We have already discussed the historical parallel between natural science and theological science, which traced the movement of thought away from a closed system of the world in Newton to a relational and fluid view in Einstein. This cosmological parallel has profound implications for the doctrine of election and offers a way forward beyond its most problematic forms.

There are those today, especially of the Calvinist perspective, who are limited by a similar outlook as the one found in Newton's mechanistic cosmology. They operate with a functional determinism, in which everything that happens is merely the causal result of a predetermined universe. God is therefore declared to be a God of pure sovereign will, merely a divine clock-maker. All events of human history are interpreted to be God's will, and these events serve God's glory *even* if they are evil and sinful occurrences. All of history may not be the direct will of God for creation, but it was nevertheless predetermined by God to serve His glory.

Calvin himself leaned towards such determinism when he wrote, "Now, since the arrangement of all things is in the hand of God, since to him belongs the disposal of life and death, he arranges all things by his sovereign counsel, in such a way that individuals are born, who are doomed from the womb to certain death, and are to glorify him by their destruction" (*Institutes of the Christian Religion,* 3.23.6). For Calvin, this means that the reprobate are destined to bring upon themselves their own destruction, while the elect are destined to rely on God's grace for salvation. As he writes in chapter 24, "[T]he wicked bring upon themselves the just destruction to which they are destined" (*Institutes,* 3.24, chapter heading). So while Calvin insists it is the reprobate's "fault" that they fall into sin and destruction, it was nevertheless preordained by God. So God does not "cause" everything, in the strict sense of the word, but everything has been predetermined to serve God's glory. It is not correct to hold Calvin to a *strict* determinism, but it is perhaps fair to say that he holds to a *functional* determinism; not every *act* itself was predetermined but certainly every *outcome* was.

While Torrance owes a debt to Calvin's theology, there remains a strong leaning towards determinism in his thought that Torrance cannot accept. This is precisely where Torrance's engagement with natural science proves to be invaluable. Our presupposed cosmology will always significantly influence our doctrine of God. If the universe is perceived to be closed and rigid, then God's interaction with us in space and time will be perceived deterministically. Newton's outlook can be seen in parallel with the determinism of Calvin's doctrine of election, which rests on the doctrine of God's absolute decree. We can free our thinking from the closed systems of both Newton and Calvin alike by learning from modern science an open and relational outlook.

Engaging in a dialogue with natural science frees us from falling into a deterministic cosmology. Such a cosmology is fundamentally incongruent with the living God proclaimed in scripture. Instead of thinking about God's abstract acts within the context of a mechanical universe, modern science sets theology free to consider the living God whose acts are made known in Jesus Christ. The question of election is no longer a question of God's absolute decree but of Jesus Christ's actual life and work, which established the relation of God and humanity as both *free* and *contingent*. Barth saw the error of Calvin's absolute decree and argued for a doctrine of election centered on Jesus Christ as God's concrete will and acts revealed in history. Likewise, Torrance's engagement with science solidifies Barth's point by critically examining this cosmological perspective as it affects the doctrine of election. (I am aware that Calvin predates Newton, so I do not mean to imply that Newton was the cause of Calvin's doctrine; but there is an undeniable similarity in their outlooks, both of which can be overcome by a better cosmology.) Future discussions of the doctrine of election which ignore this change in cosmology are bound to err on the side of determinism. Through a dialogue with natural science, theology can break free from this tendency. Because theology takes place within the created universe of space and time, we cannot do theology without also critically examining our cosmological perspective.

5

THE GROUND AND GRAMMAR OF
THEOLOGY (THE TRINITY)

SUMMARY: The doctrine of the Trinity is "more to be adored than expressed." Theology and doxology (worship) are inseparable, especially when we are talking about God's innermost being as Father, Son, and Holy Spirit. Here we are approaching the mystery of all mysteries. With humility, Torrance carefully develops the doctrine of the Trinity as the ultimate ground and basic grammar of all theological knowledge. With an emphasis on the doctrine of *perichoresis,* Torrance develops an "onto-relational" concept of personhood.

IN TORRANCE'S OWN WORDS:

I myself like to think of the doctrine of the Trinity as the *ultimate ground* of theological knowledge of God, the *basic grammar* of theology, for it is there that we find our knowledge of God reposing upon the final Reality of God himself, grounded in the ultimate relations intrinsic to God's own being, which govern and control all true knowledge of him from beginning to end.

— THE GROUND AND GRAMMAR OF THEOLOGY, 158-9

If God is not inherently and eternally in himself what he is toward us in Jesus Christ, as Father, Son, and Holy Spirit, then we do not really or finally know God at all as he is in his abiding Reality.

— REALITY AND EVANGELICAL THEOLOGY, 24

SECONDARY QUOTES:

For T. F. Torrance, the doctrine of the Trinity is *the* central doctrine around which all other Christian doctrines gravitate and become comprehensible [...] Unless theology begins from a center in God himself and unless it is controlled by the reality of God himself throughout, it becomes little more than mythology, or the projection of our human wishes based on experience on to reality, resulting in a fantasy and not perception of reality.

— PAUL D. MOLNAR: THOMAS F. TORRANCE, 31-2

INTRODUCTION

Kata physin, if we recall from chapter two, denotes the conviction that knowing in truth is knowing in accordance with the nature of the reality we seek to know. For Christian theology, this means knowledge which is fundamentally *Trinitarian,* according to God's nature as Father, Son, and Holy Spirit. If God is Triune, God must be known in a Trinitarian way. God's self-revelation in Jesus Christ defines the nature of God's being in this way, and therefore, we cannot apply foreign definitions of God's nature to God without falling into error. This is why Torrance often calls the doctrine of the Trinity the "ground and grammar of theology." This is how we must speak of God because it is how God has spoken of Godself in Jesus Christ.

In this chapter, we will examine the doctrine of the Triune God in Torrance's thought. First, as it pertains to the epistemological relevance of the Trinity, then how Torrance forms the doctrine itself, and finally we will look at Torrance's ecumenical work on the *filioque* clause (in a sidebar).

Torrance's contribution to Trinitarian theology is enormous and no single chapter can contain all of its implications. However, we will attempt to provide an overview of Torrance's essential contribution by giving a broad summary of its various developments.

BASIC GROUND AND ULTIMATE GRAMMAR

Torrance is often critical of Westminster theology, both of its Confession of Faith and its Catechism. A major reason why is that Torrance thinks Westminster theology teaches a fundamentally *divided* doctrine of God, in which the one God and the Triune God are considered separately.

All we have to do is read the Westminster Confession or Catechism to discover the truth in this claim. It is quite telling, for example, to read question number seven of the Shorter Catechism: "Question: *What is God?* Answer: God is a Spirit, infinite, eternal, and unchangeable, in his being, wisdom, power, holiness, justice, goodness, and truth." But must our answer depend so heavily on philosophical or abstract concepts? or should it not, instead, depend fully on the witness of Jesus Christ? The Christian answer should simply be: "God is the Father, Son, and Holy Spirit." This may not be the Westminster answer to "What is God?", but it is *Christ's* answer. The scriptures do not know an abstract, philosophical deity, but only the God and Father of Jesus Christ who sent the Holy Spirit to the Church. This is not to say that the answer provided in the Shorter Catechism is entirely wrong, but it does not provide an inherently *Christian* doctrine of God with its response. It constructs a doctrine of God that no longer resembles the Father of Jesus Christ because it no longer depends on Christ's witness. It resembles a speculative, philosophical doctrine of God, such as the God of the Greeks or of mythology, rather than the truly *Christian* doctrine of the Triune God revealed in Christ.

While it is true that Westminster theology affirms the doctrine of the Trinity, in actuality its affirmation is little more than superficial lip-service. The question we must ask is not: "Do you believe in the Trinity?" The essential question is, for Torrance: "Does the Trinity make up the *fundamental* truth about God, the *essential* ground and grammar of *all* theological knowledge?" For Westminster theology, it seems, the Trinity is neither fundamental nor essential, but secondary to a philosophical doctrine of the one God (via an independent natural theology). Westminster theology does not rely *wholly* on the doctrine of God's Triunity, and if you were forced to remove the Trinity from its documents, they would suffer only a slight revision. Karl Rahner summarizes this problem exceptionally well:

> We must be willing to admit that, should the doctrine of the Trinity have to be dropped as false, the major part of religious literature could well remain virtually unchanged.
>
> — THE TRINITY, 10

This is the critical problem Torrance has with Westminster theology. If the doctrine of the Trinity was one day proven false, then Westminster theology would remain "virtually unchanged"; its answer to "What is God?" would suffer no alteration. This problem reveals a startling displacement of the doctrine of the Trinity, which was at one time so essential for the Nicene Fathers, into being merely a secondary issue we affirm only superficially. Torrance calls the Church to return to its roots and discover the doctrine of the Trinity as an essential truth for the proclamation of the Gospel, as the ultimate ground and basic grammar of all our talk of God.

Westminster theology does not, however, deserve *all* the blame for this problematic outlook. It only repeats a dualism that Torrance traces all the way back to the early Church, which he sometimes calls an "Augustinian dualism." It is a dualism that Torrance believes has plagued Western theology for far too long.

This dualism separates the doctrine of the one God and the Triune God. This happens by first considering the doctrine of the one God through a series of abstract attributes (omnipotent, omnipresent, impassible, immutable, etc.) and only then by considering the doctrine of the Trinity—thus subjecting the Triune God to the philosophical notion of God's oneness. This results in a theology that is free to construct a doctrine of God on the basis of human logic and philosophical proofs, instead of depending wholly on Jesus Christ as God's self-revelation. The foundation of the former is humanity with a human-centric logic, but the foundation of the latter is God with a Christo-centric logic. Torrance thinks this is a grave error and calls us to re-think our doctrine of God with the Trinity as the "ground and grammar" of theology.

Torrance insists that if God is Triune, then the doctrine of the Trinity must make up the ground and grammar of theology; the Trinity cannot become a footnote we add onto a philosophical doctrine of the one God. There are not two ways of knowing God, one which results in the doctrine of the Trinity and the other which results in the one God. There is only one truly *Christian* doctrine of God: the doctrine of the Father, Son, and Holy Spirit—one being, three persons.

Thus, Torrance writes, "If God is triune in his nature, then really to know God means that we must know him in accordance with his triune nature from the start" (*The Ground and Grammar of Theology,* 148). If we believe, together with the whole Christian Church, that God is Father, Son, and Holy Spirit, then theology must become bound to the doctrine of the Trinity as its fundamental ground and grammar. We cannot speak of God rightly if we do not speak of God as Triune.

This conviction that the doctrine of the Trinity must be the ground and grammar of our theological knowledge follows directly from Torrance's chief epistemological claim, *kata physin*. Theological knowledge of God must be knowledge in accordance with God's very being, and therefore, it must be *Trinitarian* theology at its core, relying solely upon divine revelation and rejecting all foreign rationality incongruent with Jesus Christ. Thus, Torrance insists that if we know God, we must know God from the Father, through the Son, and in the Holy Spirit:

> To know this God, who both condescends to share all that we are and makes us share in all that he is in Jesus Christ, is to be lifted up in his Spirit to share in God's own self-knowing and self-loving until we are enabled to apprehend him in some real measure in himself beyond anything that we are capable in ourselves. It is to be lifted out of ourselves, as it were, into God, until we know him and love him and enjoy him in his eternal Reality as Father, Son, and Holy Spirit in such a way that the Trinity enters into the fundamental fabric of our thinking of him and constitutes the basic grammar of our worship and knowledge of the One God.
>
> — THE GROUND AND GRAMMAR OF THEOLOGY, 155

Knowledge of God is by grace, not works; it is as we are taken up into the self-knowing of God that we partake of the knowledge of God. God's "self-knowing" became incarnate and dwelt among us in Jesus Christ. This downward movement of grace reaching us in our estrangement is central for Torrance. Thus, he writes that to know God means being *seized* by God rather than reaching for God ourselves:

> We know God, or rather, as St. Paul put it, are known by God. We know God only in that we are seized by His reality. It is in response to that divine grasping of us that our human grasping of Him takes

place in functional dependence upon Him, as an act of 'under-standing'.

— GOD AND RATIONALITY, 22

If we attempt to grasp in ourselves the knowledge of God through an independent natural theology, then we do not arrive at the God and Father of Jesus Christ, the *Christian* God, but at an abstract deity who is in truth merely the projection of ourselves. This is why Torrance rejects all forms of natural theology which are independent of divine revelation. Natural theology begins with the highest values and truths we can think of, the "highest good," and then amplifies them to the nth degree, calling it "God." But this is fundamentally our sinful attempt to apprehend God in our own strength; it is a projection of ourselves into the heavens. We have not reached God, in reality, but have fashioned an idol after ourselves. We must be *grasped by* God in God's self-revelation, and in the process, we must repent of our self-made idols by relying solely on the Trinity as the true ground and grammar of all our theological knowledge of God. When this happens, we are lifted out of ourselves and share in God's knowledge of Godself.

There are not two ways to know God. There is only the one Christian way of knowing God: through divine revelation, as God makes Godself known in His Triunity. Torrance is convinced we must forgo all attempts to know God which do not rely wholly upon the doctrine of the Trinity. Either God is known in God's Triunity, as we are grasped by the knowledge of God shared from the Father, through the Son, and in the Holy Spirit, or God is not truly known at all—and what we are left with is merely an idolized projection of our best thoughts. The doctrine of the Trinity is what distinctly makes Christian theology *Christian*. Without it, we are resigned to mythology.

MORE ADORED THAN EXPRESSED

Now that we have clarified the importance of the doctrine of the

Trinity as the proper "ground and grammar" of all theology, we will continue to explore how precisely Torrance develops the doctrine.

Torrance begins his great work on the Trinity, *The Christian Doctrine of God*, with an explanation of method: "My argument and presentation have taken an open-structured form in the conviction that the truth of the Holy Trinity is more to be adored than expressed" (*The Christian Doctrine of God*, ix).

Torrance naturally follows the "stratified" theory of knowledge we outlined in chapter two. Theological investigation only takes place within the life of the Church, in response to the Gospel, as we humbly seek to know God as the God who has made Godself known in Christ. Torrance thinks this was the same context in which the Nicene theologians worked to overcome Arius' heresy; they wrote with a *doxological* orientation, doing theology "on their knees."

We do not come to God as spectators but as those for whom Christ died, to whom the Father pours out His love, and in whom the Holy Spirit dwells. In and through God we know God, as we participate in a saving relationship with God through Jesus Christ. We cannot form a doctrine of the Trinity abstractly, as if we might know God through impersonal observation.

Torrance's doctrine of the Trinity is built on a foundation of adoration, not on the reductionistic need to *contain* God's being with statements. The Trinity is often treated as a mathematical problem to be solved through logical analogies rather than a *mystery* we tremble before with breathless awe. This is the brilliance of Torrance's Trinitarian theology. His theological statements are left essentially *open* to the innermost being and mystery of God. He recognizes with every sentence that he can, at best, only bear inadequate witness to the great truth of God's life of love, God's incomprehensible Triunity. It is a profound sense of worship and devotion that characterizes his theological reflection.

This is a breath of fresh air in contrast with other treatments of the doctrine of the Trinity as mere historical studies of its development, or of logical, apologetic defenses of its truth. Torrance's doctrine of the

Trinity is one of my favorite aspects of his thought. It is without a doubt not only a work of masterful scholarship but of deep devotion. Torrance takes seriously the subject matter at hand, treading carefully and reminding us with every step that we truly are approaching holy ground.

> The worship and doctrine of the Trinity belong together, for it is godly thinking of God in unrestrained awe and adoration of his unfathomable Triune Nature that must guide any move toward formulating a doctrine of the Trinity in terms worthy of him.
>
> — IBID., 75

Without a posture of worship, the doctrine of the Trinity deteriorates into empty speculation.

A REVOLUTION IN OUR KNOWLEDGE OF GOD

Only through Jesus Christ do we know God. Therefore, Torrance begins with divine revelation:

> Only in Christ is God's self-revelation identical with himself, and only in Christ, God for us, does he communicate his self-revelation to us in such a way that authentic knowledge of God is embodied in our humanity, and thus in such a way that it may be communicated to us and understood by us.
>
> — THE CHRISTIAN DOCTRINE OF GOD, 1

Torrance is quick to point out that this does not mean all theology "can be reduced to Christology, but that because there is only one mediator between God and man, the Man Christ Jesus, in the presentation of the doctrines of the Christian faith, every doctrine will be expressed in its inner coherence with Christology at the centre, and in its correspondence with the objective reality of God's self-revelation in Christ" (ibid.). Therefore, the doctrine of Christ and the doctrine of the Trinity are inseparably joined together, so that one cannot be considered apart from the other. The doctrine of the Trinity makes up the "innermost heart of Christian faith and worship, the central dogma of classical theology, the fundamental grammar of our knowledge of God" (ibid., 2).

The doctrine of the Trinity is not just *a* doctrine among other doctrines. For Torrance, the doctrine of the Trinity is *the* doctrine which makes Christian theology truly *Christian*. The Trinity expresses the core of the Christian faith, apart from which there is no Gospel. Torrance writes:

> The doctrine of the Trinity enshrines the essentially Christian conception of God: it constitutes the ultimate evangelical expression of *the Grace of the Lord Jesus Christ* who though he was rich for our sakes became poor that we through his poverty might become rich, of *the Love of God* who did not spare his own Son but delivered him up for us all, for it is in that personal sacrifice of the Father to which everything in the Gospel goes back, and of *the Communion of the Holy Spirit* through whom and in whom we are made to participate in the eternal Communion of the Father and the Son and are united with one another in the redeemed life of the people of God. Through Christ and in the Spirit God communicated himself to us in such a wonderful way that we may really know him and have communion with him in his inner life as Father, Son and Holy Spirit.
>
> — IBID.

Thus, Torrance declares: "This self-revelation of God in the Gospel amounts to the greatest *revolution in our knowledge of God*" (ibid., 3). This great revolution in our knowledge of God is what Torrance pursues by placing the doctrine of the Trinity central to his doctrine of God. We cannot go back to the old dualism between the one God of philosophical knowledge and the Triune God of revelation. There is no use mixing non-Christian notions of God with Christian ones; the doctrine of the Trinity draws a line in the sand. It is the defining characteristic of what it means to confess Jesus Christ as Lord. There is simply no room for a doctrine of God that is not fundamentally Trinitarian. Accordingly, Torrance writes:

> It is not just that the doctrine of the Holy Trinity must be accorded primacy over all the other doctrines, but that properly understood it is the nerve and centre of them all, configures them all, and is so deeply integrated with them that when they are held apart from the doctrine of the Trinity they are seriously defective in truth and become malformed. Moreover, if the Christian conception of God and of all his activity toward us in creation and redemption is essentially trinitarian, then the trinitarian perspective must be allowed to pervade all Christian worship and practice, all interpretation of the Holy Scriptures, and all proclamation of the Gospel, and must be given a regulative role in the dynamic structure of all Christian thought and action. Then indeed we will live and move and have our being under the blessing of the Grace of the Lord Jesus Christ, the Love of God and the Communion of the Holy Spirit.
>
> — IBID., 31

This is the heart of what Torrance pursues in describing the doctrine of the Trinity as the basic ground and fundamental grammar of our knowledge of God, and it is why Torrance stressed so often the errors of Western dualism. If we take the Trinity seriously, and not offer mere lip-service to its truth, then we have the makings of a revolution in our doctrine of God.

God "loves us more than He loves Himself"

Torrance next considers God *for us* (the economic/evangelical Trinity) and God *in Godself* (the ontological/theological Trinity). He writes of their inherent unity, "In the Gospel God does not just *appear* to us to be Father, Son and Holy Spirit, for he really *is* Father, Son and Holy Spirit in himself, and reveals himself as such" (*The Christian Doctrine of God*, 7). While we should distinguish God's external acts (*God for us*) from God's inner being (*God in Godself*), we cannot separate the two. Who God is for us *is* who God is in Godself.

Therefore, we come to learn that God is not "some abstract impersonal essence, but *dynamic personal being*, for God is who he is in the Act of his revelation, and his Act is what it is in his Being" (ibid., 4; emphasis mine). The dynamic personal being of God acting for us in the person and work of Jesus Christ makes known God's innermost being. This is why Torrance often called the cross an "open window" into the heart of God, for "it is in the Cross of Christ that the utterly astonishing nature of the Love that God is has been fully disclosed, for in refusing to spare his own Son whom he delivered up for us all, God has revealed that he loves us more than he loves himself" (ibid., 5).

This is a startling statement that Torrance often repeats, and therefore, it is worth examining briefly. For Torrance, the incarnation was a genuine *risk* for God. Torrance insists we recognize that God hazarded His very existence as God in the incarnation by risking the central bond of the Father and the Son. The Son entered an *anti*-God world, our world, and took up our fallen, rebellious humanity as His own. By taking up our sinful humanity, the scriptures say Jesus was *tempted* in all things (Heb. 4:15). We can have no illusions that Jesus lived a struggle-free life. Day after day the Son of God fought from within our fallen existence to maintain the essential bond He shared with His Father in the Holy Spirit. The very relationship that makes God *God* was at risk. Yet Jesus did not sin or rebel against His Father, He remained faithfully obedient in spite of our rebellious humanity. By living out this obedience *as a human* before the Father, the Son of God converted our corrupt humanity back to fellowship with God. For Torrance, this is why the incarnation is *itself* already a work of atonement (though it is not the *only* aspect of the atonement). It also explains why Torrance makes the startling claim that God "loves us more than he loves himself," however contradictory it may sound. God truly *risked* Godself, in selfless love for us, by sending the Son of God into an anti-God world, into our fallen existence.

FATHER, SON, AND HOLY SPIRIT

The incarnate Son did not become a human being apart from the inner bond constituting His very being as God; truly, the whole life and fellowship of God tabernacled among us (John 1:14). It was the Son *only* who became a man, but it was precisely the Son *of* the Father in the Holy Spirit, the Son who is not Son apart from the fellowship of the Father in the Holy Spirit. There is no *isolated* Son any more than there is an isolated Father or Holy Spirit. The Triune God came to us through the incarnation, even if it was the Son alone who became incarnate. Since this Father/Son/Spirit relationship constitutes the essential being of God, we cannot imagine the incarnation of the Son without His inseparable bond with the Father in the Holy Spirit.

This is expressed well by two quotations from St. Athanasius, which are key for Torrance's doctrine of the Trinity:

> It would be more godly and true to signify God from the Son and call him Father, than to name God from his works alone and call him Unoriginate.
>
> — ATHANASIUS: CONTRA ARIANOS, 1.34; CITED IN
> TORRANCE: TRINITARIAN FAITH, 49

> He who calls God Father, signifies him from the Son, being well aware that, since there is a Son, it is of necessity through the Son that all things that have come into being were created. When they [the

Arians] call him Unoriginate, they name him only from his works, and do not know the Son any more than the Greeks. But he who calls him Father, names him from his Word and, knowing the Word, acknowledges him to be the Maker of all, and understands that through him all things come into being.

— ATHANASIUS: CONTRA ARIANOS, 1.33; CITED IN
TORRANCE: IBID., 77

When we call the Father "Father" of the Son and the Son "Son" of the Father we do so in a precisely theological way. We do not indicate God by the works of God but describe the very being of God when we say Father, Son, and Holy Spirit. This is not a name we apply to God ourselves but God's very own self-revelation.

As such, there is no Father without the Son or Son without the Father, and neither exist without the communion of the Holy Spirit. Their fellowship constitutes God's innermost being, and therefore, each person exists and is defined only in relation to the others. As Torrance writes:

Each Person is intrinsically who he is for the other two. They coinhere in one Another by virtue of their one Being for Another and by virtue of the dynamic Communion which they constitute in their belonging to one Another.

— THE CHRISTIAN DOCTRINE OF GOD, 133

This is why we cannot speak of the Son except as the Son of the Father in the Holy Spirit. The person of the Son of God *is* who He is as the Son *dwelling in* and *for* the Father and the Holy Spirit. The Son's very identity is bound to this fellowship which makes up the Godhead. As Torrance further clarifies:

The Father is not properly Father apart from the Son and the

Spirit, and the Son is not properly Son apart from the Father and the Spirit, and the Spirit is not properly Spirit apart from the Father and the Son, for by their individual characteristics or distinctive properties as Father, Son and Holy Spirit, they exist in and through one Another and belong to and ever live for each Other.

— IBID., 132-3

We cannot speak of the Son apart from the Father or the Spirit, because, as Gregory of Nazianzen famously said:

No sooner do I consider the One than I am enlightened by the radiance of the Three; no sooner do I distinguish them than I am carried back to the One. When I bring any One of the Three before my mind I think of him as a Whole, and my vision is filled, and the most of the Whole escapes me. I cannot grasp the greatness of that One in such a way as to attribute more greatness to the rest. When I contemplate the Three together, I see but one Torch, and cannot divide or measure out the undivided Light.

— ORATIONS, 40.41; CITED IN TORRANCE: THE
CHRISTIAN DOCTRINE OF GOD, 112

At the heart of this, we discover a doctrine known as *perichoresis,* which we will now consider more fully.

PERICHORESIS

We've been describing the doctrine of *perichoresis* already, though without naming it directly. For Torrance, the doctrine of *perichoresis* articulates a radical change in what it is to be a person, especially what it means *for God* to be "three persons." The doctrine of *perichoresis* "helps us to develop a careful theological way of interpreting the biblical teaching about the mutual indwelling of the Father and the Son and the Spirit" (*The Christian Doctrine of God*, 102).

The word itself is borrowed from the Greek. *Chora* means "space" or "room," and *chorein* means "to make room." As such, *perichoresis* "indicates a sort of mutual containing or enveloping of realities, which we also speak of as *coinherence* or *coindwelling*" (ibid.). This is the inter-penetration of the Father, Son, and Holy Spirit, mutually co-inhering and co-indwelling one another (John 14:20). This inter-penetration is what makes up their very personhood. We do not define the three persons of the one being of God with a humanistic under-standing of personhood but must learn precisely what personhood means for God. As Colin Gunton writes, "Torrance moves from peri-choresis to person and not the other way around, arguing that *by virtue of* the concept of perichoresis there developed a new concept of the person in which 'the relations between persons belong to what persons are'" (*The Promise of Trinitarian Theology*, 125).

While the word *perichoresis* does not directly appear in scripture, it was nevertheless a term defined by the Church for a specialized theo-logical purpose, that is, to better describe the biblical content. Accord-ingly, it is an essential term for Trinitarian theology, as Torrance writes:

> It was then applied to speak of the way in which the three divine Persons mutually dwell in one another and coinhere or inexist in one another while nevertheless remaining other than one another and distinct from one another. With this application the notion of *perichoresis* is refined and changed to refer to the complete mutual containing or interpenetration of the three divine Persons, Father, Son and Holy Spirit, in one God.
>
> — THE CHRISTIAN DOCTRINE OF GOD, 102

God's very being as personal being is being in communion, being in the mutual interrelation and interpenetration of Father, Son, and Holy Spirit. As we have said, the Father is not Father apart from the

Son, nor the Son without the Father, and neither the Father nor the Son is without the Holy Spirit. With the doctrine of *perichoresis* in mind, we can see precisely why this is true. God's very being is being in communion. Torrance goes so far to write, "With God, Being and Communion are one and the same" (ibid., 104). In fierce contrast against the impersonal gods of Hellenistic culture, the Christian doctrine of God is fundamentally personal, because what constitutes the very being of God is the co-inherent communion of the persons of the Father, Son, and Holy Spirit. Torrance emphasized this by writing:

> No divine Person is who he is without essential relation to the other two, and yet each divine Person is other than and distinct from the other two [...] The relations between the divine Persons belong to what they are as Persons—they are constitutive onto-relations. 'Person' is an onto-relational concept.
>
> — IBID., 157

Torrance coins the term "onto-relations" to adequately describe this new concept of personhood. The term indicates that the ontological being of each person is constituted by their relation to another. This is what Torrance means when he says a person is an "onto-relational concept."

We often define personhood in terms of *isolation,* but this is the opposite of what theological language means when describing God as "one being, three persons." In the light of the *perichoresis,* we have to see the term "person" as a *technical* term which cannot be casually defined through creaturely understanding. Persons, in Trinitarian theology, are strictly *perichoretical* persons, persons who co-inhere in one another, "onto-relational" persons whose very personhood is made up of a relationship with other persons.

Coming to understand God's personal being in the light of onto-relational personhood redefines what it means for the Father, Son, and Holy Spirit to be persons. It also redefines how human beings are *meant* to be persons, even if this is rarely how we see personhood. We are persons not in isolation from others but our very personhood is constituted by the relationships we keep. I am not a human being in isolation from others: I am a son, a husband, and a friend. I would not be who I am without these relationships, for they constitute my identity as a human being.

The idea of "onto-relational" personhood could have profound ramifications for our violently individualistic culture. It would enact an enormous change in our social structures if we properly understood our personhood in terms of our relations to others and not merely in terms of our relation to ourselves. We might learn to love our neighbors again and see the bigger picture that no human being lives in isolation, that the suffering of some is the burden of all.

Social implications aside, the important lesson is that we cannot define personhood through our fallen human existence, but we must let God redefine personhood according to Godself. We must learn from God's being, as it is expressed so well with the doctrine of *perichoresis,* what true personhood is.

The images of "Father" and "Son" refer to the truth of God's being, but they refer to it in such a way that creaturely content is excluded. There is no "grandfather" of the Father, nor was the Son created by the Father, as Torrance writes:

> We may not read the creaturely content of our human expressions of 'father' and 'son' analogically into what God discloses of his own inner divine relations. Hence Gregory Nazianzen like Athanasius insisted that they must be treated as referring *imagelessly,* that is in a diaphanous or 'see through' way, to the Father and the Son without the intrusion of creaturely forms or sensual images into God.
>
> — THE CHRISTIAN DOCTRINE OF GOD, 158

The terms "Father" and "Son" refer imagelessly to the truth of God's being. We do not define these terms but allow the truth of God's reality to be the ultimate definition. Theology must reason with a center in God, thinking only in accordance with God's self-revelation, and not with a center in ourselves. This is made clear in the doctrine of *perichoresis,* which redefines true personhood and gives us a better understanding of what we mean when we say God is "one being, three persons."

GOD IS LOVE

A helpful way to understand *perichoresis* is within the context of God's being as love, that God *is* love. "This is what the doctrine of the Holy Trinity supremely means, that God himself is love" (*The Christian Doctrine of God,* 162). God's love is not a static, lifeless love in which God merely "is" without the dynamic act of loving, but God's love is, fundamentally, the inter-personal love of the Father, Son, and Holy Spirit. This is why Augustine attempted to understand the Trinity by their inter-loving relations, as the *Lover,* the *Loved,* and the *bond of Love* (*On the Trinity,* Book IX). If God in Godself *is* love, then God's very being is dynamic and Trinitarian—not static, unmoved, passionless, or solitary.

Torrance illustrates well this dynamic Trinitarian love of the Father, Son, and Holy Spirit:

Through the *coming* of Jesus Christ into the world as the only begotten Son loved by the Father, the Love which flows eternally between the Father and the Son in the Holy Trinity has moved outward to bear upon us in history and is made known to us above all in the sacrificial love of Jesus in laying down his life for us. And in the *ascending* of Jesus Christ to the Father the Love of God embodied among us in him and exhibited to us in his incarnate life and sacrifice, is shown to be grounded in the eternal Love of God the Father, the Son, and the Holy Spirit in their mutual indwelling in the Holy Trinity. The Love of God revealed to us in the economic Trinity is identical with the Love of God in the ontological Trinity;

but the Love of God revealed to us in the economic manifestation of the Father, the Son and the Holy Spirit in the history of our salvation, tells us that God loves us with the very same love with which he loves himself, in the reciprocal love of the three divine Persons for Each Other in the eternal Communion of the Holy Trinity.

— IBID., 165

This describes the other-giving, other-centered being of God, the *perichoresis* of the Triune God, turned outwards to humanity in selfless love. The very same love that God is in Godself, the love of the Father to the Son in and through the Holy Spirit, is the same love God pours out on fallen humanity in the incarnate life and work of the Son. God was love before the creation of the world, and it is out of His being as love that the universe came to be. God will be love for all eternity, and it is to share in the love God is in Godself that is the ultimate joy of human beings in union with Jesus Christ.

The interpenetrating love of the Holy Trinity is the context for Jesus' "high-priestly" prayer in the Gospel of John. This prayer is an appropriate concluding summary for Torrance's doctrine of the Trinity:

As you, Father, are in me and I am in you, may they also be in us, so that the world may believe that you have sent me. The glory that you have given me I have given them, so that they may be one, as we are one, I in them and you in me, that they may become completely one, so that the world may know that you have sent me and have loved them even as you have loved me.

— JOHN 17:21-23, NRSV

SIDEBAR: THE FILIOQUE CLAUSE

The *filioque* clause is, in part, behind one of the oldest splits in the Christian Church, the 1054 "Great Schism" of East and West. Western theologians added the clause to the Nicene Creed, much to the dismay of Eastern theologians. It is perhaps Torrance's greatest contribution to Trinitarian theology that he worked for a way beyond this thousand-year-old impasse. It is at the very least Torrance's most important *ecumenical* contribution, which naturally follows from his conviction that, "A theology that is not essentially ecumenical is a contradiction in terms" (*The School of Faith,* lxviii).

What is the *filioque* clause? The original Nicene Creed reads, "I believe in the Holy Spirit, the giver of life, who proceeds from the Father. Who with the Father and the Son is adored and glorified." Western Theologians added a second procession of the Spirit to the end of the first sentence, so that it reads, "I believe in the Holy Spirit [...] who proceeds from the Father *and the Son.*"

This simple addition caused tremendous controversy between the Eastern and Western expressions of Christianity. Classic arguments for and against the clause are summarized well by Gary W. Deddo:

The West, in order to protect the divinity of the Son, altered the ecumenical Niceno-Constantinopolitan Creed by expanding the clause which said the Spirit proceeds from the Father by adding the word 'and the Son' (*filioque*). The Eastern Church claims this 'double procession' threw the unity of the Godhead into disarray for now it seemed that there were two sources or founts for the spiration of the Holy Spirit.

— THE PROMISE OF TRINITARIAN THEOLOGY, 89

There are valid theological reasons both for and against the *filioque* clause. On the one hand, it is necessary that the doctrine of procession affirms the divinity of the Son; but, on the other hand, a double procession implies two sources of the Spirit or two "beings" in God from whom the person of the Spirit proceeds. This, in part, helps explain the impasse between Eastern and Western theology, though of course history is never quite so simple. Generally speaking, however, this is the core problem behind the inclusion or exclusion of the *filioque* clause. We will move on to explore how Torrance navigates the controversy and offers an ecumenical way forward for both the Western and Eastern Churches.

TORRANCE'S CONTRIBUTION

Torrance finds the *filioque* clause *unnecessary* and *misleading*. In its place, Torrance offers an alternative phrase. This is the proposition that the Holy Spirit proceeds "from the Father *through* the Son." Do not let the simplicity of this solution fool you, there is tremendous theological depth to it.

Essential to this proposal is a renewed understanding of what's sometimes known as the divine "monarchy." The Cappadocian theologians "tended to locate the unity of the Godhead in the mon-arche (*monarchia*) of the Father, at times speaking of the *person* of the Father as the cause and source of the being of the Son and Spirit [...] This way of putting it seemed to suggest that the divinity of the Son and the Spirit was derived" (Deddo, *The Promise of Trinitarian Theology,* 89).

In contrast with the traditional doctrine of divine monarchy, Torrance argues we must apply the doctrine of *perichoresis* to the personal being of God. Accordingly, the relations of the Father, Son, and Holy Spirit must not be understood in terms of *cause and effect* but in terms of *perichoretic communion.* Instead of attributing the divine monarchy to the *person* of the Father, making the Father the source of the Son and the Holy Spirit, Torrance thinks a *perichoretic* understanding of the *being* of God finds the source of the Son and the Holy Spirit not in the *person* of the Father but in the *being* of God in *perichoresis.* This makes it possible to set aside the problems inherent in the *filioque* clause and move beyond them.

Deddo again offers a helpful summary:

The unity of Trinity must not be located in the person of the Father, but in the perichoretic Triunity of the being of God. The being of the Spirit does not proceed from the person of the Father, but rather the person of the Spirit proceeds from the person of the Father who, in his being, is in communion with the Son, i.e., in the communion that the Spirit is. In this frame, the deity of all the Persons is clearly underived. All the persons have their being by being perichoretically and enhypostatically Triune. Thus the Unity in being of God is none other than a Triunity [...]

In this way the unity of the Godhead is secured without inadvertently being open to the charge of subordinationism or a hierarchy within the Godhead while the divinity of the Son is secure without inadvertently leaving the unity of the Godhead vulnerable to conceptual deteriorations. It was in this way that agreement was reached between the two branches of the Church on the procession of the Spirit.

— IBID., 90

Colin Gunton offers this summary:

> In effect Torrance is saying that the solution is to be found in the doctrine that the procession, coming as it does from the being of the Father rather than from his person, involves the whole of the Godhead in such a way that a choice between the two positions should not be required.

— IBID., 129

By moving the monarchy from the *person* of the Father to God's personal *being* in *perichoresis,* Torrance makes obsolete the *filioque* clause. Torrance moves beyond the impasse with his proposal of the Spirit's procession from the Father *through* the Son. Since the person-hood of Father, Son, and Holy Spirit are constituted as *perichoretical,* personhood-in-relationship, or onto-relational persons, then the question of procession is to be thought "not in any partitive way but only in a holistic way, as procession from the completely mutual relations within the one indivisible being of the Lord God who is Trinity in Unity and Unity in Trinity" (Torrance: *Trinitarian Perspectives,* 113).

Western theologians no longer need to include "and the Son" to the procession of the Holy Spirit to protect the Son's divinity, because the Son co-inheres with the Father. The procession of the Spirit from the Father *implies* the divinity of the Son since it is from the Father *through* the Son that the Spirit proceeds (because the Father is not Father without the Son). The *filioque* clause is deemed unnecessary and misleading in the light of a proper understanding of the personhood of the Father as an "onto-relational" person, in whom the Son co-inheres together with the Holy Spirit.

Eastern theologians would likely be satisfied by this proposal, because, since a *perichoretic* understanding of the Father implies procession from the Father *through* the Son, the *filioque* clause becomes unnecessary. The monarchy of the Trinity is no longer applied to the *person* of the Father but to the *personal being* of God understood perichoretically.

ECUMENICAL AGREEMENT

All of this is rather technical, but a summary of Torrance's doctrine of the Trinity would be incomplete without making note of this significant contribution. Deddo has called it "perhaps Torrance's greatest contribution to the life of the church" (*The Promise of Trinitarian Theology*, 107). The ramifications are vastly theological, but profoundly ecumenical as well. Unifying the Eastern and Western perspectives in this way, Torrance was able to spearhead a remarkable and historic joint agreement on the doctrine of the Trinity between the Orthodox Church and the World Alliance of Reformed Churches in 1991.

There were three key statements in the joint agreement that Torrance had a hand in developing. The first involves a personalizing of the being of God. The second moves the divine monarchy from the person of the Father to the one being of God shared by all three persons according to the doctrine of *perichoresis,* thus excluding the notion of subordination. And finally, the procession of the Spirit "from the Father *through* the Son" was agreed upon, since this retains the unity of the Godhead and the divinity of each person. The Holy Spirit then proceeds from the Triune *being* of the Godhead (understood perichoretically) and not solely from the *person* of the Father. Ultimately, this makes unnecessary the *filioque* clause.

Torrance writes reflectively, summarizing these three points as they were agreed upon by both the Orthodox and Reformed Churches:

(1) In formulating their agreement the two theological commissions insisted that the historic trinitarian formula 'One

Being, Three Persons' must be understood in a wholly personal way. It has often been held that while the Father, the Son and the Holy Spirit are personal, the one Being of God common to the three Persons is not. That unbiblical idea has been completely set aside. The doctrine of 'One Being, Three Persons' does not rest on any preconceived idea or abstract definition of the divine Being, but on the very Being of God as he names himself 'I am who I am / I shall be who I shall be', the one ever-living and self-revealing God. That God is a fullness of personal Being in himself is made known to us in the Gospel through the one self-revealing act of God the Father, the Son and the Holy Spirit. Thus in the doctrine of the Holy Trinity the 'One Being' of God does not refer to some abstract divine essence, but to the intrinsically personal 'I am' of God [...]

(2) Of far-reaching importance is the stress laid by The Agreed Statement on the 'Monarchy' of God, or the one ultimate Principle of Godhead, in which all three divine Persons share equally, for the whole indivisible Being of God belongs to each of them as it belongs to all of them. This is reinforced by a deepened understanding of the way in which the three divine Persons indwell, interpenetrate and contain one another [*perichoresis*], while remaining what they are in their different properties and distinctness as Father, Son and Holy Spirit. Any notion of subordination in the Trinity is completely ruled out, as is any notion of degrees of Deity among the divine Persons, such as between 'the underived Deity of the Father', and 'the derived Deities of the Son and the Spirit'.

(3) The doctrine of the one Monarchy of God which may not be restricted to one divine Person, together with that of the complete interpenetration of the three divine Persons in one another within the one indivisible Being of the Holy Trinity, means that the procession of the Spirit from the Father must

be considered in the light of the indivisible unity of the Godhead in which each Person is perfectly and wholly God. The effect of this is to put the doctrine of the procession of the Spirit on a fully trinitarian basis. Clearly more thought must be and will be given to this, but, as I understand it, the fact that the One Being of God the Father belongs fully to the Son and the Spirit as well as to the Father tells us that the Holy Spirit proceeds ultimately from the Triune Being of the Godhead. Does this not imply that the Holy Spirit proceeds from out of the mutual relations within the One Being of the Holy Trinity in which the Father indwells the Spirit and is himself indwelt by the Spirit? This approach is reinforced by the truth that, since God *is* Spirit, 'Spirit' cannot be restricted to the Person of the Holy Spirit but applies to the whole Being of God to which the Father and the Son with the Holy Spirit belong in their eternal Communion with one another. This deepening of the concept of the procession of the Spirit from the *Being* of God the Father is drastic and far-reaching, for it breaks through the traditional formalisations within which East and West have been divided

— (TRINITARIAN PERSPECTIVES, 111-13)

The ecumenical and theological implications of Torrance's contribution to Trinitarian theology are without a doubt of great importance for continued dialogue. While it is highly technical and at times difficult to understand, this is an element of Torrance's thought that we simply cannot ignore because it is perhaps one of his most significant and far-reaching contributions to theology today.

6

THE TWOFOLD AGENCY (MEDIATION) OF CHRIST

SUMMARY: Jesus Christ is at once God for humanity and a human being for God. This is the twofold agency (mediation) of Christ, in which Christ acts both *Godward* and *humanward*. Therefore, Christ mediates the things of God to humanity and the things of humanity to God.

IN TORRANCE'S OWN WORDS:

In [Jesus Christ] the revealing of God and the understanding of man fully coincided, the whole Word of God and the perfect response of man were indivisibly united in one Person, the Mediator

— THE MEDIATION OF CHRIST, 9

Jesus Christ is Mediator in such a way that in his incarnate Person he embraces both sides of the mediating relationship. He is God of the

nature of God, and man of the nature of man, in one and the same
Person.

— IBID., 56

Undoubtedly, Hebrews 3:1 was one of Torrance's favorite biblical
verses. He cited it often: Jesus Christ is 'the apostle and high priest of
our confession.' Christ is the faithful apostle. In him God has uttered
himself. Christ is also the obedient man. As Jesus the human has
heard and answered God.

— ANDREW PURVES: EXPLORING CHRISTOLOGY AND
ATONEMENT, 212

INTRODUCTION

A unique aspect of Torrance's theology is his emphasis on the twofold
agency of Christ. This boils down to a conviction that Jesus Christ acts
at once humanward and Godward, that is, both as God *towards*
humanity and as a human being *towards* God in twofold mediation.
The hypostatic union, the doctrine that Jesus Christ is fully God and
fully human without confusion or division, becomes a *dynamic* movement in which Christ's life is seen as the point of contact between all
humankind and God. Here we will explore a few of the notable
insights of Christ's twofold agency, as well as some of its practical
implications.

THE WORD THAT REACHED US

The Word of God is not like a rock thrown aimlessly from on
high, nor is it an indifferent proclamation, unworried if we understand
it or are changed by it. Torrance has avoided precisely this by empha-

sizing the Godward and humanward agencies of Christ because here he grounds the Word of God in our true humanity. God's Word is not an abstract Word we must discover on our own; it is the Word that has truly *reached* us in the depths of our darkness, which has sought us out and found us. It is not a shout into the void of human existence. Torrance writes:

> [W]e have to do with the Word of God only as it has been addressed to us and has actually reached us, Word that has called forth and found response in our hearing and understanding and living—otherwise we could not speak of it. We do not begin, then, with God alone or with man alone, nor even with God speaking on the one hand and man hearing on the other hand, but with God and man as they are posited together in a movement of creative self-communication by the Word of God. This is not Word in which God exists only in and for Himself or which He speaks to Himself alone, but Word by which He creates and upholds other realities around Him and gives them room for their relations with Him [...] The nature of the reciprocity is such that in assuming human form the Word of God summons an answering movement from man toward God which is taken up into the movement of the Word as a constitutive part of God's revelation to man. Thus the Word of God communicated to man includes within itself meeting between man and God as well as meeting between God and man, for in assuming the form of human speech the Word of God spoken to man becomes at the same time word of man in answer to God.
>
> — GOD AND RATIONALITY, 137-8

Not only has God's Word reached us in our actual humanity but, from within the depths of our existence, God has found true *reciprocity*. Jesus Christ is the one true mediator of God and humankind, mediating both the cause of God to humanity and the cause of humanity to God. The incarnation was not a one-sided event,

God alone speaking to human beings, but includes the Son of God *as a human being* acting on our behalf before the Father, receiving and responding to God's Word in our place. The Son was not merely the Word *proclaimed* to us but at once the human *response* to God's Word. In this we discover the mediation of Christ, both on the side of God and of all humanity, as Torrance continues to explain:

> This is Jesus Christ, the Interpreter and Mediator between man and God, who, as God of God in unqualified deity and as Man of man in unqualified humanity, constitutes in the unity of His incarnate Person the divine-human Word, spoken to man from the highest and heard by him in the depths, and spoken to God out of the depths and heard by Him in the highest. He is not only the Word of God come to man and become man, but He who as man bears and is the Word of God, the Word not only as God utters it but the same Word as heard, uttered and lived by man, and who as such carries in Himself the vicarious actuality, and conveys in Himself the active possibility, of true and faithful response on the part of all men to God's Word. It is thus in the form of sheer humanity in all its lowliness, weakness and darkness that God's Word has reached us and made provision for free and adequate response on our part, but in such a way that far from being a dispensable medium to be discarded as soon as the target is reached, the humanity of the Word, God's condescension to be one with us in our humanity, remains the proof that in His own eternal Being He is not closed to us, and the manifestation of His freedom to unveil Himself to man and share with him His own divine Life.
>
> — IBID., 138-9

Classically, theology has given little more than lip service to a doctrine known as the "hypostatic union." This is the doctrine that Jesus was both God and a human being without confusion or separation. For Torrance, this union was a *dynamic* relationship and not merely a static one. In Christ, it was not a neutral humanity that was united to God, but it was precisely *our* humanity that God assumed. As such, Jesus Christ is the true mediator for both God to humanity and as a human before God. This is a dynamic relationship between the divine and human natures of Christ, without confusion or separation. Jesus Christ *as God* reaches humanity, and Jesus Christ *as a human* hears and responds to God's Word in faithful obedience. This is not two movements of two persons but the one person of Jesus Christ, one movement in this twofold form.

Following Athanasius, Torrance insists that Jesus "ministered not only the things of God to man but ministered the things of man to God" (*Theology in Reconciliation,* 228). As our brother, bone of our bone and flesh of our flesh, Jesus Christ acted as the high priest of all creation, ministering human concerns to God *as a fellow human being.* Torrance writes:

> Jesus Christ the Word of God has become man, has assumed a human form, in order as such to be God's language to man, and that in Jesus Christ there is gathered up and embodied, in obedient response to God, man's true word to God and his true speech about God. Jesus Christ is at once the complete revelation of God to man and the correspondence on man's part to that revelation required by it for the fulfilment of its own revealing movement.
>
> — THEOLOGY IN RECONSTRUCTION, 129

This reciprocity of the divine and human in Christ is an important Christological insight, though one theology has often ignored. Torrance emphasized this Godward and humanward movement of Christ throughout his work, and, as we will see in the next chapter, it led to one of his most important and practical doctrines: the vicarious humanity of Christ. For now, we will continue by exploring this dynamic twofold movement in the history of Israel.

ISRAEL: THE WOMB OF THE INCARNATION

Israel holds an important place in Torrance's understanding of the incarnation, especially here in terms of Christ's mediation. For Torrance, the history of Israel tells the process of God's painful, but necessary, molding of a people-group into the "womb" of the incarnation. Their culture and history were chosen so that God's Word might be made known to humanity; so that His Word might be *received* in human existence and truly *reach* us. Torrance writes:

> That is what happened between God and Israel, for the Word of God spoken to man did not operate in a vacuum but penetrated human existence in the particular life and history of one people elected as the instrument for the actualization of God's revelation in humanity and separated as a holy nation in whose midst God dwelt in an intimate way through the presence of His Word. The covenant relationship between God and Israel which this set up was a particularization of the one covenant of grace which embraced the whole of creation and constituted its inner bond and ground, and therefore carried in it the promise of a final universalization of God's revelation in which His Word would bring light and salvation to all the peoples of mankind and indeed a new heaven and a new earth.
>
> — GOD AND RATIONALITY, 147

God elected the people of Israel to "actualize" the revelation of God in humanity. As Torrance rightly points out, the Word of God cannot come to us in a vacuum devoid of history and culture. If God's Word has truly *reached us,* then it must reach us as we are in our actual existence. This means molding the thoughts and culture of a particular people to establish a place for God's Word to be received and understood. This is apparent in the history of Israel. God fought against the pagan notions which attempted to influence their understanding and taught Israel time and time again that God is not like the gods of other nations, that there is no God but YHWH. Throughout their history, God taught the Israelites to know the true God from the false gods of other nations, and therefore, in their culture and history, God established a place where His self-revelation could be received. Torrance writes:

> God has adapted Israel to His purpose in such a way as to form within it a womb for the incarnation of the Word and a matrix of appropriate forms of human thought and speech for the reception of the incarnational revelation. And so Jesus was born of Mary, out of the organic correlation of Word and response in the existence of Israel, to be the Word of God made flesh in the life and language of man and to be that Word heard and expressed in the truth and grace of perfect human response to God. In Him God's Word has become speech to man through the medium of human words and speaks to men as man to man, for in Him God has graciously assumed our human speech into union with His own, effecting it as the human expression of the divine Word, and giving it as such an essential place in His revelation to man.
>
> — IBID., 149

Israel was God's witness among the nations. This theme is often explored in the Old Testament, and it culminates in the incarnation of Jesus Christ: God *as* an Israelite in self-witness. Without the Jewish people and culture, we could not have understood the Word of God when it came to us; it would have been like a rock thrown down from above without explanation or context. Through Israel, however, we can understand God's Word so that it does not fall on deaf ears. This is why Torrance calls Israel the "womb" of the incarnation since their history paved the way for Christ's coming.

Israel's role in God's self-revelation was not *only* as a womb for the incarnation—as if Israel has no *lasting* significance. The history of Israel also provides the context for Jesus' life and ministry. Torrance stresses, "Thus to detach Jesus from Israel or the incarnation from its deep roots in the covenant partnership of God with Israel would be a fatal mistake" (*The Mediation of Christ*, 23). Israel remains essential for understanding God's self-revelation, as Torrance continues:

> We have tried to understand Jesus within the patterns of our own various cultures so that in the West and the East we have steadily gentilised our image of Jesus. We have tended to abstract Jesus from his setting in the context of Israel and its vicarious mission in regard to divine revelation [...] We desperately need Jewish eyes to help us see what we cannot see because of our gentile lenses, that is, the culture-conditioned habits of thought and interpretation which we bring to Jesus and which make us read into him the kind of observational images which have played such a dominant role in our literary culture and, until recent decades, in our scientific culture as well.
>
> — Ibid., 19-20

The Word of God purposefully assumed *Jewish* flesh, not just any flesh. This makes the history and culture of Israel the proper context for understanding Christ's life and ministry. Without Israel and its role in the incarnation, we would not have understood the Word of God when it came to us. Therefore, Israel remains the essential context for the Word of God.

THE MIND OF CHRIST

We must go to school with Israel and share with it the painful transformation of its mind and soul which prepared it for the final mediation of God's self-revelation in Jesus Christ, if we ourselves are to break free from our assimilation to the patterns of this world and be transformed through the renewing of our mind in Christ, for only then will we be in a position to recognise, discern and appreciate what God wills to make known to us.

— THE MEDIATION OF CHRIST, 12

Jesus Christ is the full actualization of the knowledge of God in our humanity. The human *mind* of Jesus knows God *as a human,* and in Him, we share in His knowledge of God. Paul wrote, "We have the mind of Christ" (1 Cor. 2:16). So it is by *grace* that we participate in the mind of Christ, it is a gift. It is not a goal pursued but a given reality we participate in by the Holy Spirit.

This does not mean, however, that we are automatically *aligned* with the mind of Christ. We are still called to think in accordance with Jesus, to renew our minds, and "go to school with Israel." Torrance often called the humanity of Christ the "real text of the New Testament Scriptures," because "He is God's exclusive language to us and He alone must be our language to God" (*God and Rationality,* 151). We are compelled to think of God exclusively in terms of Jesus Christ, to participate in His knowledge of the Father in the Holy Spirit.

At the heart of the twofold agency of Christ is His human mind which knows God on our behalf. In union with Him, we rightly respond to the Word of God, and by grace, we participate in God's knowledge of Godself. This displaces our religious attempts to respond to God in and of ourselves and forces us to rely wholly upon Jesus Christ as the one true mediator between God and humanity. We cannot respond to God's grace in our own strength but are justified through the faithfulness of the Son of God.

Grace does not negate our natural humanity but perfects and completes it in the vicarious mind of Christ. In the next chapter, we will explore more fully the "vicarious" nature of Christ's humanity, in which He acts in faithful obedience on our behalf towards the Father and in the Holy Spirit.

SIDEBAR: THE BIBLE AS WITNESS

Related to the twofold agency of Christ is the twofold nature of the scriptures. The Bible is at once God's Word spoken to fallen humanity but spoken precisely in and through the words of fallen human beings. As Torrance writes, "Holy Scripture is assumed by Christ to be his instrument in conveying revelation and reconciliation, and yet Holy Scripture belongs to the sphere where redemption is necessary" (*Theology in Reconstruction,* 138).

Both the human and divine aspects of the Bible are important to consider. Here Torrance avoids both the errors of liberal and conservative doctrines of scripture. Conservatives tend to make the Bible a perfect divine oracle, bordering on the heresy of Docetism, while liberals tend to make the Bible a human book of religious history or existential consciousness, bordering on the heresy of Ebionitism. Torrance holds together both the divine and human characteristics of the Bible in his doctrine of scripture.

The Bible is not a book of "ready-made" truths free from the burden of exegesis and hermeneutics. This is often the mistake inerrantists make when they identify biblical statements, which bear *witness* to the truth, with the truth itself. It is important to distinguish between the divine and human aspects of the Bible but not to *remove* the unavoidable human element. The human element cannot be ignored, as Torrance writes:

> We are not concerned here with the Word of God *in abstracto,* i.e., in abstraction from the [human medium], but we are concerned with the Word of God *in concreto,* in the actual human situations in which the Word has addressed itself to men in the Old Testament and in the New Testament, in and through the actual humanity with which the Word has wrestled, achieving within it, in spite of its recalcitrance and intractability, an obedient instrument for its revealing purpose.
>
> — THEOLOGY IN RECONSTRUCTION, 141

We cannot fall prey to the opposite error of reading the Bible as a purely human book with only human things to say to us. We should have a healthy understanding of the humanity of the Bible but never at the cost of removing all divine content from its text. Torrance writes from the perspective of this error:

> We are not concerned here, however, with the human speech of the Bible as an independent theme of study, that is, with the humanity of the original witness in themselves, all of whom without exception point away from themselves to the Word of the Lord which has laid hold upon them and drawn them within its saving operation.
>
> — IBID., 142

Stressing both the humanity of the Bible and its divinity, the human words which speak the Word of God, is essential for the doctrine of scripture. Neither side of the equation should be excluded. The scriptures are neither purely divine nor purely human, but God's Word speaking through the medium of human words. Just as Jesus Christ in His life and work is at once humanity to God and God to humanity, so the Bible is both God's perfect Word to humanity and the words of imperfect human beings through which we hear God's Word.

For Torrance, therefore, "[T]he Holy Scriptures are the *spectacles* through which we are brought to know the true God" (*Reality and Evangelical Theology*, 65). The Bible bears *witness* to the truth of God's reality; its statements do not *contain* the truth in themselves. They are "true," but they are not "the Truth." It is by looking *through* the statements of scripture that we can see the truth which its statements bear witness to. By looking through the lens of scripture we come to see God's self-revelation in Jesus Christ and, in the Holy Spirit, come to a loving fellowship with the Triune God. We do not look *at* the Bible for its own sake but look *through* its statements to encounter the truth of Jesus Christ. Failing to distinguish between the statements themselves and the truth the statements point to would be like trying to read a book by examining a pair of reading glasses. We must look *through* reading glasses to read, not fixate on the glasses themselves. The Bible is a *tool*, a necessary means to an end, but not an end unto itself.

Torrance is often critical of this fundamentalist tendency to confuse statements which indicate truth with the truth in itself:

At this point the epistemological dualism underlying fundamentalism cuts off the revelation of God in the Bible from God himself and his continuous self-giving through Christ and in the Spirit, so that the Bible is treated as a self-contained corpus of divine truths in propositional form endowed with an infallibility of statement which provides the justification felt to be needed for the rigid framework of belief in which fundamentalism barricades itself.

— IBID., 17

The result of "closing-off" statements of the Bible from the truth of God to which they refer is "to give an infallible Bible and a set of rigid evangelical beliefs primacy over God's self-revelation which is mediated to us through the Bible" (ibid.). By mistakenly identifying "biblical statements of truth with the truth to which they refer," fundamentalists focus more on the *statements* of truth rather than on the *truth* its statements point us towards. This ultimately results in turning the Bible into a protestant "paper pope" (Barth's phrase). Biblical infallibility attempts to justify statements of truth *apart from* the truth to which its statements refer. Therefore, inerrancy attempts to make the statements of the Bible a self-contained foundation for truth, thus removing its statements from the foundation of Jesus Christ who *is* the truth. As such, it is a form of self-justification.

Instead, we should understand the Bible as pointing away from itself, under the leading of the Spirit of Truth, to Jesus Christ Himself. The biblical statements do not exhaustively contain God's truth but indicate more than what can be reduced to words. Since the scriptures point away from themselves to the truth, they are not "the" truth in themselves (even though they are "true"). Understanding the Bible as a *pointer* or *witness* is important to balance the divine and human aspects of the Bible. We cannot force the Bible to become some kind of divine oracle, perfectly containing in itself all truth. Nor can we reduce the Bible down to its humanity. Instead, we must let the Bible serve its purpose, to bear witness in human words to the self-revelation of God. Instead of focusing on the *accuracy* of the statements themselves, as if the truth of God depended on the truth of a book, we should focus instead on looking through the scriptures to the truth of God's reality. These are *human* words, yes, but they are God's Word *in* and *through* human words.

In this regard, Torrance thinks the Bible is *necessarily inadequate* precisely *because* its witness is true. He writes on statements of truth, "[I]t must be said that their inadequacy in this way is an essential part of their truth, in pointing away from themselves to the truth they serve, as it is an essential element in their objectivity in being grounded beyond themselves on reality that is independent of them" (ibid., 51).

The point is not that there are any specific errors in the Bible but that all language, when speaking of God, is necessarily inadequate. The Bible is a *human* book bound to the limitations of human speech just as much as it is *God's Word* speaking in spite of its limitation. A purely divine oracle would be an inhuman witness, and as such, it would not reach us in our actual condition as human beings bound to the limitations of our time and culture. In a similar way that Israel was necessary for the incarnation, so the humanity of the Bible is necessary for its faithful witness to God's divine Word. This does not give us permission to go on a witch hunt for errors in the Bible, but it means we can no longer find assurance (self-justification) in the absolute perfection of a book.

The Bible is God's chosen witness. For this reason alone we trust its ability to faithfully speak God's Word through the Holy Spirit's leading. Our faith is not in the adequacy or independent perfection of the Bible but in the God who uses the weak and foolish things in the world to shame the strong and the wise (1 Cor. 1:27). If this is how God works among us, why would the Bible be any different? God's strength is perfected in weakness (2 Cor. 12:9). Through the Holy Spirit, the inadequate human witness of scripture becomes God's own Word, God's own witness. If we follow Paul's logic, we should recognize that it is in the *weakness* (humanity) of the Bible that we discover its strength: "I will boast all the more gladly of my weaknesses, so that the power of Christ may dwell in me" (2 Cor. 12:9, NRSV).

7

THE VICARIOUS HUMANITY OF CHRIST

SUMMARY: Jesus lived *as a human* united to His Father, reconciling our humanity to God through His vicarious life of perfect faith, obedience, and prayer. The Christian life in all its aspects has been taken up in His life lived in our name and on our behalf. Our faith is understood rightly as an echo of His faith, sustained and made perfect in Him. We are set free from the burden of looking over our shoulders and worrying if we have "enough" faith; what little faith we have has been taken up and perfected in Christ. This is Torrance's doctrine of the "vicarious humanity" of Christ.

IN TORRANCE'S OWN WORDS:

We are to think of the whole life and activity of Jesus from the cradle to the grave as constituting the vicarious human response to himself which God has freely and unconditionally provided for us... Jesus Christ is our human response to God. Thus we appear before God and are accepted by him as those who are inseparably united to Jesus

Christ our great High Priest in his eternal self-presentation to the Father.

— THE MEDIATION OF CHRIST, 80

He assumed all that was ours in the experience of our human life in body, mind and soul, including human prayer and worship, that he might offer himself to the Father on our behalf and in our place, and present us sanctified and renewed in and through himself to the Father.

— THEOLOGY IN RECONCILIATION, 156

SECONDARY QUOTES:

Torrance maintains that the Word of God incarnate in Jesus Christ not only delivered humanity from subjugation to sin and alienation, but also recreates humanity's relation to God by realizing perfect humanity on the earth, offering God the *true human response* to God on our behalf and in our place, which we cannot make for ourselves.

— ELMER E. COLYER: HOW TO READ T.F. TORRANCE, 110

INTRODUCTION

When the Gospel calls men and women to repentance and faith, it is not the call for an independent work performed in order to earn God's acceptance. Yet this is far too often implied—as if grace were some sort of *transaction* between us and God. God has supplied X and Y, but it is still up to us to supply Z to complete the work. That is, we are thrown back upon ourselves to muster up the right amount of faith or repentance. Torrance does not deny the necessity of rightly responding to God, but Torrance brilliantly *displaces* us as the focal point of our personal responses. Jesus Christ as a human being responded to the Father in perfect faith and repentance. *Christ* is the focal point of the human response to God, and our personal responses are made only *within* His response, as an *echo* to His vicarious humanity.

In the last chapter, we discussed the twofold agency of Christ in its humanward and Godward movement. In this chapter, we will continue that discussion, focusing especially on Christ's life as a human before the Father, to explore Torrance's doctrine of the "vicarious humanity" of Christ. We will also discuss this doctrine in relation to Torrance's work on the sacraments since it is there that the practical effects of the doctrine are seen most clearly.

PERSON AND WORK

It is important that we never separate the work of Christ from His person. There simply is no saving work of Christ without equal recognition of His saving life. The life of Christ is the only proper context for His death. His death was not just *any* death; it was significant precisely because it was *His* death.

One of Torrance's chief grievances against Western theology is its tendency to fall prey to this error by either directly or indirectly separating Christ's work from His person. Torrance thinks this wrongful dualism *externalizes* the Gospel, turning the death of Christ into an empty, legalistic transaction. Why is it so essential that we think together the person and work of Christ? Torrance writes:

> It was not the *death* of Jesus that constituted atonement, but Jesus Christ the Son of God offering Himself in sacrifice for us. Everything depends on *who* He was, for the significance of His acts in life and death depends on the nature of His person. It was *He* who died for us, *He* who made atonement through His one *self*-offering in life and death. Hence we must allow the Person of Christ to determine for us the nature of His saving work, rather than the other way round. The detachment of atonement from incarnation is undoubtedly revealed

by history to be one of the most harmful mistakes of Evangelical
Churches.

— GOD AND RATIONALITY, 64

The Gospel is not the announcement of a possible transaction
between human beings and an impersonal deity; although, whenever
the work of the Gospel is made external to the person of Jesus Christ
this is a natural conclusion. Here faith and repentance are mistaken as
an "admittance fee" to grace. Torrance's emphasis on the vicarious
humanity of Christ rightly stresses the unconditional nature of grace in
the face of our legalistic tendencies. Without this emphasis, we would
inevitably be thrown back upon ourselves to complete the Gospel.

Torrance often referred to Calvin's insistence that we will never
find a "naked" Christ, a Christ without His promises, but only "Christ
clothed with His Gospel." Likewise, Torrance argues we cannot think
of Christ's work for our salvation apart from His vicarious life lived on
our behalf. The person and work of Christ cannot be separated. There
is no "naked work" of Christ without the vicarious life of Christ, nor is
there a life of Christ which does not culminate in His work.

The problem with an externalized Gospel is that Jesus Christ does
not remain essential for every aspect of our salvation since the person
of Christ has been marginalized. We know that we are saved only
because of Jesus, but we lack a firm understanding of Christ's life as
the essential foundation for our Christian lives. We cannot live an
independent Christian life apart from Christ any more than we can
save ourselves. If salvation is merely a transaction that puts us "in the
black" before God, yet the Christian life lived in fellowship with God
remains *our duty* to uphold, then Jesus is merely a tool God used to
save us from sin that is no longer needed for the life we now live in
Him. Torrance comments on this tendency within the context of
Christ's benefits:

It is only through union with Christ that we partake of His benefits, justification, sanctification, etc. [...] Apart from Christ's incarnational union with us and our union with Christ on that ontological basis, justification degenerates into only an empty moral relation.

— IBID., 64-5

Union with Christ is essential for Torrance's understanding of salvation. We are not reconciled to God through an external transaction, as if Christ can be discarded after His saving work is made complete. Justification is not achieved *apart* from Him but only in union with Him. When we separate Christ's person from His work, we separate His *benefits* from His person. The Christian life becomes a work we are left to complete in ourselves, not a life lived exclusively in and through union with Jesus Christ.

As an example, Torrance points out how the Westminster Confession of Faith reversed the order of Calvin's original doctrine of justification. For Calvin, "We must possess Him: for His blessings are not ours, unless He gives Himself to us *first*" (Calvin's Catechism, cited in Torrance, ibid., 64). For Calvin, union with Christ comes first and only, as a result, do we partake of His benefits. However, the Westminster Confession "reversed the order of things: we are first justified through a judicial act, then through an infusion of grace we live the sanctified life, and grow into union with Christ. The effects of this have been extremely damaging in the history of thought" (ibid., 65).

The difference is startling. Calvin and Torrance rightly understand union with Christ as the first and central aspect of the Christian life, but Western theology has made it into a conclusion earned by good works. Torrance thinks this is the result of separating the person of Christ from His work and therefore the benefits of Christ from His person. The work of Jesus Christ must not be separated from His person, and by failing to understand this, we turn the Christian life into a life lived apart from Him. Jesus becomes a *tool* in God's hands that is later set aside after its purpose is complete. The critical difference is whether or not Christ remains central, remains the foundation, not just in the work of atonement but for all aspects of salvation, including the Christian life.

Torrance traces the damaging effect of this error:

> Not only did it lead to the legalizing, or (as in James Denney's case) a moralizing of the Gospel, but gave rise to an 'evangelical' approach to the saving work of Christ in which atonement was divorced from incarnation, substitution from representation, and the sacraments were detached from union with Christ; sooner or later within this approach where the ontological ground for the benefits of Christ had disappeared, justification became emptied of its objective content and began to be re-interpreted along subjective lines. It is because this is the state in which so many people in this country [Scotland] find themselves today that they become such easy prey for the reductionist notions of the Gospel that reach us from the Continent [i.e., the so-called fundamentalists in America]. We Protestants require to go back in our tracks in order to recover something we lost in our reaction against Roman error, how to interpret the work of Christ from His Person rather than the other way round. Unless we do that we will inevitably interpret both the work and the person of Christ from out of ourselves.

> — GOD AND RATIONALITY, 65

When we preach the Gospel only in terms of its benefits, we miss the point. The Gospel is not a list of things God offers us in exchange for our faith and allegiance to Him. The Gospel *is* Jesus Christ. The chief benefit of salvation is not freedom from sin or an escape from hell; it is ultimately *fellowship with God.* God is both the means *and* the end of our salvation. We focus too often on the benefits of salvation that we miss Jesus Himself who is its benefit.

We do not live the Christian life by our own strength. Paul made this clear enough when he wrote, "I have been crucified with Christ;

and it is no longer I who live, but it is Christ who lives in me" (Gal. 2:19-20). If the work of Christ for our salvation is separated from His saving person, then the Christian life deteriorates into a series of external works and religious efforts. With a firm focus on Christ's vicarious humanity, we return to a fuller understanding of salvation by grace alone.

THE COVENANT FULFILLED

What is the "vicarious humanity" of Christ? Simply put, it is the faith, obedience, worship, prayer, repentance, and life of the Son of God lived as a human being before the Father on our behalf. He fulfills our human response to the Father by perfectly doing what we cannot do: living a life of true fellowship with God from within our sinful humanity. It is helpful to think of this in terms of the covenant.

There are always two sides to a covenant, but we often imagine that God's covenant with humanity depends on *our* faithfulness to God. We imagine that we are held responsible to complete the "human side" of the covenant, whether it is by good works, faith, repentance, or a righteous Christian life. But this is precisely the problem with thinking in terms of an externalized Gospel that separates Christ's work from His person. We will never properly live in obedient faithfulness before God. "Our side" of the covenant cannot depend one iota on our abilities or else the Gospel is not good news.

In our place, Jesus Christ takes up "our side" of the covenant and perfectly lives a life of faithfulness and obedience to His Father as a human. In Him, the covenant is completed from the side of God to humanity *and* from the side of human beings in response to God. Any response that we make to God is a response made from within the humanity of Christ, upheld and sustained by the one who perfectly lived a life of obedient faithfulness on our behalf before the Father. This is the saving significance of Christ's life.

This means that we are not thrown back upon ourselves to respond to God's work of salvation, but that we rely wholly on Jesus Christ's perfect response on our behalf. We are not left to fearfully wonder if we have had "enough" faith, if we have properly repented enough, if our worship is acceptable to God, if our prayers are said rightly, if we attend Church enough, if we read the Bible enough, or if we love God enough. The humanity of Jesus Christ *is* our perfect response, which has already been offered by Christ and accepted by God. We rely on His response and echo a response only within His obedient humanity.

You can see how radically different this is from the "externalized" Gospel so criticized by Torrance. Rather than postulating a kind of "Gospel transaction," Torrance emphasizes the truly *finished work* of God's grace. It is not only complete from the side of God but at once from the side of humankind in and through the humanity of Christ.

This does not mean we are passive subjects acted on without our knowledge, participating in a salvation "over our heads" that does not truly reach us in our daily lives. By emphasizing the vicarious humanity of Christ, Torrance does not exclude our personal responses to God but sees them taken up *in* and *with* Christ's response in our humanity. Christ's vicarious life does not replace our life, but it means our life is lived rightly only *in Him*. The Christian life is not built *on its own foundation* but on Christ. In Him, we participate in the Triune life of God, as we are lifted beyond our human capacity to participate in His relationship with the Father.

Torrance comments on the way Athanasius navigated this distinction, and the same could be applied to Torrance's own theology:

> For the great Athanasius, however, godly contemplation and humble worship of the Holy Trinity, and the reverent formulation of the doctrine of the Trinity [...] had the effect of making him concentrate his personal faith all the more squarely upon the vicarious humanity of Christ who identified himself with us in our lost and corrupt existence in order to heal and redeem us and restore us to participation through the Communion of the Spirit in the eternal Life and Love of God.

— THE CHRISTIAN DOCTRINE OF GOD, 111

For Torrance, the vicarious humanity of Christ does not remove the need for personal faith but calls us to concentrate what little faith we have on the perfect faithfulness of the Son of God. He lived vicariously for us, faithfully responding to the Father's love as a man among us and reconciling us to God. We participate in His fellowship with God; we are not thrown back upon ourselves to perfectly live a life of faithfulness in our own strength. We still live before God, but it is *in Him* that we truly live and move and have our being. That He has done it all on our behalf does not mean we are left with nothing to do, but that in Him and through His life we live unto God without fear. Our response to God's grace does not *depend* on us, but neither does it *exclude* us.

Imagine a young child holding onto her father's hand as they walk across the street. Is it really the child holding onto her father's hand, or is it not the father who is ultimately holding onto his daughter's hand? Who is finally responsible for their connection? The father, of course, has the stronger grip, and his grip *upholds* the weak grasp of his daughter. The father's hand guides and encompasses his daughter's. Their connection does not depend on the strength of her grip. He will hold onto her even if her grip falters and grows weak.

The same is true for the vicarious humanity of Christ. What matters is not the strength of *our* response to God, of our faith or obedience. What matters is *Christ's* life lived on our behalf. The father's grip is stronger than the child's, just as Christ's strength upholds our holding onto Him. We are sustained and upheld in the safety of Christ's faithfulness before the Father. This image is not a perfect analogy for what Torrance is describing, but it is a helpful picture to keep in mind as we continue.

VICARIOUS LIFE

We must think of Jesus as stepping into the relation between the faithfulness of God and the actual unfaithfulness of human beings, actualising the faithfulness of God and restoring the faithfulness [of] human beings by grounding it in the incarnate medium of his own faithfulness so that it answers perfectly to the divine faithfulness. Thus Jesus steps into the actual situation where we are summoned to have faith in God, to believe and trust in him, and he acts in our place and in our stead from within the depths of our unfaithfulness and provides us freely with a faithfulness in which we may share [...] That is to say, if we think of belief, trust or faith as forms of human activity before God, then we must think of Jesus Christ as believing, trusting and having faith in God the Father on our behalf and in our place.

— THE MEDIATION OF CHRIST, 82-3

FAITH

Our faith is upheld within the faithfulness of Jesus Christ, as He responds to the Father on our behalf. Faith is certainly an important aspect of the Christian life, but it is not *our* faith that is essential. Jesus Christ believed for us. We are not thrown back upon ourselves to have faith but are called to rely wholly on Him. As Torrance writes:

Jesus Christ is the Truth of God actualized in our midst, the incarnate faithfulness of God, but He is also man keeping faith and truth with God in a perfect correspondence between His life and activity in the flesh and the Word of God [...] If it was in His humanity in entire solidarity with us that Jesus Christ stood in our place, and gave to God an account for us in His life and death, in utter faithfulness to God and to man, then this includes the fact that He believed for us, offering to God in His vicarious faithfulness, the perfect response of human faith which we could not offer.

That is what the Word of God proclaims to us in the Gospel, and therefore it summons us to respond by faith only as it holds out to us free participation in the faithful response of Christ already made on our behalf. Hence our response of faith is made within the ring of faithfulness which Christ has already thrown around us, when in faith we rely not on our own believing but wholly on His vicarious response of faithfulness toward God. In this way Christ's faithfulness undergirds our feeble and faltering faith and enfolds it in His own [...].

— GOD AND RATIONALITY, 154

Whenever a preacher tells their congregation to "have faith" and "grow in their faith," without a firm understanding of *Christ's faith* on our behalf, they have turned faith into a work. Jesus Christ *is* perfect faith. He has acted faithfully before the Father vicariously. Christ has thrown a "ring of faithfulness around us," and it is only *within* His faith that we have faith and believe God. Christ takes up our feeble faith and "enfolds it in His own," taking the burden of having enough faith off our shoulders. When faith is understood objectively as Jesus Christ's faith from within our humanity, and subjectively as our echoed faith upheld in His faith, then divine grace returns the center of the Gospel.

Torrance was fond of quoting Galatians 2:20 to articulate the vicarious faith of Christ, though he insisted on a particular way the text should be translated. He argues that it is not properly rendered, "I live by faith *in* the Son of God," but that it more accurately reads, "I live by the faith *of* the Son of God." For Torrance, it is not faith *in* the Son of God that is essential but the faith *of* the Son of God on our behalf.

Torrance is not incorrect in translating the passage this way. Most reputable translators will offer "the faith *of* the Son of God" as an alternative translation inherent to the original Greek (and many have already rendered "*of* the Son of God" primary, such as the KJV and NRSV). But the Church suffers from a lack of understanding *Christ's* faith as the foundation for our faith, so most translators have chosen "I live by faith *in* the Son of God" by default (NIV, NASB, ESV, MSG). Torrance is not, however, going against what the original Greek says but is highlighting an important insight from the text. When we consider this verse together with the whole context of Paul's letter, it should not be read as if *our* faith in Christ is essential, but that the faithfulness of the Son of God on our behalf is what matters most (see further Paul in Eph. 4:11-13).

The point of Paul's frequently quoted statement in Galatians simply cannot be that *we* live by *our* faith in Christ. For Paul, *we* have been crucified with Christ. Whatever feeble faith we attempt to muster up out of our own strength has been put to death in Him. Our life is now hidden with Christ in God (Col. 3:3). The only faith we can depend on is the perfect faithfulness of Jesus Christ on our behalf. We have absolutely no self-generated faith apart from Christ's faith. His faith is the foundation and source of our faith. If we live before God, it is only by the faith *of* the Son of God. This is of decisive importance for Torrance.

WORSHIP

Worship is the "natural expression of faith" (*God and Rationality*, 156). But worship is not best understood as a work we perform, because it is fundamentally an "expression of faith in its objective orientation in the humanity of Christ, rather than subjective self-expression on the part of believers" (ibid.). Worship is objectively the loving faithfulness of the Son towards the Father in the communion of the Holy Spirit. It is in *this* Trinitarian fellowship that we participate as we join in Christ's vicarious worship, not merely our own subjective, independent worship apart from the humanity of Christ. Worship is not primarily a human expression but an echo of the fellowship of love and trust that God is in Godself.

God's Word "establishes our communion with God in the crea-turely freedom that obtains between human speaking and responding, and summons us to formulate our human responses to Him within that freedom" (ibid., 157). It is from *within* the response of Jesus Christ on our behalf that we freely respond in worship to God, participating in the Triune adoration of the Son towards the Father and in the Holy Spirit. We do not worship from a foundation we have built up for ourselves but only in and through the humanity of Jesus. Central to this is understanding the "priestly" office of Christ as both priest *and* offering. When we come to God in worship it is neither in our own name (as our own priests) or with our own offering, but in Christ's name and with His offering on our lips. Torrance writes:

> He fulfilled in Himself the Word of God tabernacling among men, the covenanted way of response to God set forth in the ancient cult, and constituted Himself our Temple, our Priest, our Offering and our Worship. It is therefore in His name only that we worship God, not in our own name, not in our own significance but solely in the significance of Christ's eternal self-oblation to the Father.
>
> — IBID., 158

There is a subtle, yet severe form of pride that has entered our modern understanding of worship. We have wrongly displaced Christ by making ourselves the center of the whole affair. *Our* offerings and *our* praises have become more important than the royal priesthood of Jesus Christ. This becomes apparent if we consider what a fine line there is between a worship leader and a "celebrity" personality. Worship leaders with record deals and high-end production costs are not necessarily a bad thing in and of themselves, but if these things displace the central fact that *our* offering is insignificant apart from Christ's offering before the Father, then they act more as a stumbling block to true worship than as a catalyst for it. True worship is worship in the name of the Son, in and through whom we participate in the Triune life of God. Jesus Christ is the one true worship leader. False worship is worship in our own name. True worship displaces us and refocuses our attention on the mutual love of the Triune God, the fellowship that God is in Godself. We participate in God's loving communion when we worship in the name of Jesus, but sadly, it is more common in the Church today to worship in the name of our favorite worship bands than in the name of Jesus Christ. The Church needs a new expression of worship with the humanity of Jesus Christ at its center. We will regain a richer understanding of worship—an understanding free from semi-Pelagian tendencies or the idolization of personalities—when we return our focus to Christ who alone is the one true priest and offering. Truly, Jesus is the only worship leader of the Church.

T. F. Torrance's brother, James B. Torrance, has written an excellent book on this subject: *Worship, Community and the Triune God of Grace.* James explains exceptionally well the vicarious nature of Christ's worship, writing:

> Christ takes what is ours (our broken lives and unworthy prayers), sanctifies them, offers them without spot or wrinkle to the Father, and gives them back to us, that we might 'feed' upon him in thanksgiving [...] Christian worship is [...] our participation through the Spirit in the Son's communion with the Father, in his vicarious life of worship and intercession. It is our response to our Father for all that he has done for us in Christ. It is our self-offering in body, mind and spirit, in response to the one true offering made for us in Christ, our response of gratitude (*eucharistia*) to God's grace (*charis*), our sharing by grace in the heavenly intercession of Christ. Therefore, anything we say about worship—the forms of worship, its practice and procedure—must be said in the light of him to whom it is a response. It must be said in the light of the gospel of grace.
>
> — J. B. TORRANCE, 15

The point isn't to remove any human element from worship, putting ourselves out of the equation entirely, but to return the humanity of Jesus Christ and His communion with God to the center of our offering. Christ takes what little faith, love, devotion, worship, and obedience we have to give God, and He sanctifies it in His perfect response to the Father on our behalf. We are not thrown back upon ourselves to worry whether or not our offering is enough, whether or not we have believed enough or truly acted righteously. We are thrown upon the mercy of Jesus Christ who alone acts in our place perfectly before the Father. We are secure in Him, without fear or shame, and included in the very communion of God.

The Gospel is not about what we must do for God but about what God has done for us. Rather than shouting, "Repent or perish!", in the face of a lost and broken world, we proclaim a message of hope and joy, that "Christ has repented and perished for your sake!" In Him, God has acted *as a human being* in order to lift human beings up into fellowship with the Triune God. This is truly good news, an announcement that does not throw poor sinners back upon themselves in hopelessness, but which lifts every burden and brings unspeakable joy.

THE SACRAMENTS

Torrance's work on the sacraments is a notable aspect of his thought, but it is especially insightful for examining the vicarious humanity of Christ. George Hunsinger once called Torrance's work "the most creative Reformed breakthrough on the sacraments in twentieth-century theology, and arguably the most important Reformed statement since Calvin" (*The Promise of Trinitarian Theology*, 143). Essentially, Hunsinger thinks the brilliance of Torrance's work is that it brings together the positions of Calvin and Barth on the sacraments. Hunsinger explains:

> The immense contribution of Thomas F. Torrance to an understanding of the sacraments in the Reformed tradition can be appreciated in this setting. What Torrance accomplishes is, in effect, to bring Calvin and Barth together into a brilliant new synthesis.

Like Calvin (but unlike Barth), Torrance sees baptism and the
Lord's Supper as forms of God's Word, establishing and renewing
the Church in its union and communion with Christ. Like Calvin,
that is, he sees the sacraments as vehicles of testimony that impart
the very Christ whom they proclaim (by the gracious operation of
the Holy Spirit), as opposed to Barth, who insisted on seeing them
'ethically' as no more than grateful human response to a prior
divine grace not mediated or set forth by the sacraments themselves
[...]

However, like Barth (but unlike Calvin), Torrance has an
unambiguous grasp on how salvation must be spoken of essentially
in the perfect tense. He thereby uses a consistently Christocentric
soteriology to 'disambiguate' [remove uncertainty from] [...] Calvin's
view of the sacraments.

— IBID., 142-3

Ultimately, for Torrance, "It is the reference to Christ's humanity
that is crucial" (Hunsinger, ibid., 143). The vicarious nature of Christ's
humanity is central to Torrance's understanding of the sacraments, as
Torrance himself explains:

Both Baptism and Eucharist are acts of human response to the
proclamation of God's Word, but they are above all the divinely
appointed and provided ways of response and worship. They are not
sacraments of what we do but Sacraments of the vicarious obedience
of Christ once and for all offered in His finished work, and for ever
prevalent before the Face of the Father in the heavenly intercession
and mediation of His Son.

— GOD AND RATIONALITY, 158

This moves the sacraments away from merely being a religious duty
or personal obligation to a celebration for what God has done for us in

Christ. Torrance does this by emphasizing our joyous participation in the incarnate life of Jesus Christ through the sacraments:

> The primary *mysterium* or *sacramentum* is Jesus Christ himself, the incarnate reality of the Son of God who has incorporated himself into our humanity and assimilated the people of God into himself as his own Body, so that the sacraments have to be understood as concerned with our *koinonia* or participation in the mystery of Christ and his Church through the *koinonia* or communion of the Holy Spirit.
>
> — THEOLOGY IN RECONCILIATION, 82

This is a *twofold* participation, both as we participate in Christ and as Christ participates in our humanity. This is why Torrance can say that baptism "is to be understood as referring not simply to the baptising of someone in the name of Christ but to the baptism with which Jesus Christ himself was baptised for our sakes in the whole course of his redemptive life from his birth to his resurrection" (ibid., 83). When we are baptized, we are baptized in the baptism of Jesus Christ. Christ was baptized for our sakes in the Jordan river, which foreshadowed His descent (immersion) into death and His rising again. (Paul makes this connection between Christ's baptism and death, and us together with Him, in Rom. 6:1-11.) Christ's vicarious baptism, in water and grave, is the "material content and active agent" of our baptism in Him. It is *Christ's* baptism that we are baptized into. It is not an empty ritual with mere *reference* to Christ, but truly it is His vicarious baptism and sacrificial death that we partake of in the sacraments.

This emphasis on Christ's vicarious humanity frees us to respond to God without fear since we are enclosed in His perfect response already made on our behalf and accepted by God. As Torrance writes:

> The Sacraments provide the natural basis within our daily physical

existence for free and spontaneous response to the Word of God in which we do not have to keep looking over our shoulders to see whether our response is good enough. The very fact that in our response we are called to rely entirely upon the steadfast and incorruptible response of Christ made on our behalf frees us from the anxieties begotten of ulterior motivation and evokes genuine freedom and joy in our responding to God.

— IBID., 159

Christ's vicarious humanity frees us from relying upon the adequacy of our efforts. This calls into question the thought that we might somehow "mess up" the sacraments. I grew up with a fear that if I ever went to the Lord's Supper with an impure heart I would be "cursed." I remember vividly the warnings of my childhood pastor not to come to the table if I was not ready in my heart to receive it. Torrance's perspective is extremely practical. We are free from looking over our shoulders for fear of not doing enough or being good enough for God. The responsibility of a perfect response is not ours to bear, Christ has taken the burden upon Himself.

Hunsinger writes further about the twofold participation of Torrance's doctrine of baptism:

As Christ communicates himself to us in baptism, so he also joins us at the same time to himself. Therefore, as we receive him into our hearts, we are also drawn at the same time into living participation in him.

— THE PROMISE OF TRINITARIAN THEOLOGY, 145

This follows the logic of Irenaeus, who, as Hunsinger notes, referred to baptism as "the sacrament of the incarnational reversal" (ibid.). This moves the sacrament of baptism away from being merely a dry ritual and returns it to its rightful place as the joyous celebration of our inclusion and participation in the life of God. Torrance writes at length on baptism:

> Jesus was baptised with the baptism of repentance not for his own sake but for ours, and in him it was our humanity that was anointed by the Spirit and consecrated in sonship to the Father [...] He received the baptism meant for sinners. In our human nature he received the divine judgement upon sin; in our human nature he made atonement, and in our human nature he rose again from the dead. When he was born, died and rose again, it was our human nature which was born, died, and rose again in him... For us, baptism means that we become one with him, sharing in his righteousness, and that we are sanctified in him as members of the messianic people of God, compacted together in one Body in Christ. There is *one baptism* and *one Body* through the *one Spirit.* Christ and his Church participate in the one baptism in different ways—Christ actively and vicariously as Redeemer, the Church passively and receptively as the redeemed Community [...]
>
> Hence the baptism of individual people is to be understood as their initiation into and sharing in the one vicarious *baptisma* of Christ. Through his birth they have a new birth and are made members of the new humanity. Through his obedient life and death as the incarnate Son their sins are forgiven and they are clothed with a new righteousness. Through his resurrection and triumph over the powers of darkness they are freed from the dominion of evil. Through his ascension to the Father the Kingdom of Heaven is opened for them, and they wait for his coming again to fulfil in them the new creation. Through sharing in his Spirit they are made members of his Body and are admitted into the communion of the Holy Trinity.

As an ordinance, then, baptism sets forth not what we do, nor primarily what the Church does to us, but what God has already done in Christ, and through His Spirit continues to do in and to us.

Torrance's understanding of the Lord's Supper also contains this emphasis on the vicarious humanity of Christ. For Torrance, "[T]he key to the understanding of the Eucharist is to be sought in the *vicarious humanity of Jesus, the priesthood of the incarnate Son*" (ibid., 110). Torrance quotes Athanasius approvingly, "He became Mediator between God and men in order that he might minister the things of God to us and the things of ours to God" (*Contra Arianos,* IV). The *continual* nature of this mediation is important for Torrance. Not only during Christ's life on earth but in all eternity before the Father, Jesus Christ is a *human being* now and forever mediating the cause of human beings in the midst of the Trinity. In union with Him, we participate in His communion with God. We take part in Christ's status before God when we partake of in the Lord's Supper, as Torrance writes:

> It is in this union and communion with Christ the incarnate Son who represents God to us and us to God that the real import of the Lord's Supper becomes disclosed, for in eating his body and in drinking his blood we are given participation in his vicarious self-offering to the Father. As we feed upon Christ, the bread of life who comes down from above, eating his flesh and drinking his blood, thereby receiving his eternal life into our actual life, and living by Christ as he lived by the Father who sent him, he unites us and our worship with his own self-consecration and so offers us to the Father in the identity of himself as Offerer and Offering.

Torrance again brings to mind Galatians 2:20. The Pauline phrase, "I live, yet not I... I live by the faithfulness of the Son of God" should "apply to our worship in Christ as much as to our life in

Christ, for what God accepts as our true worship is Christ himself" (ibid.).

Like baptism, the Lord's Supper should not be regarded as an independent offering *apart from* the offering of Jesus Christ. Instead, this is an act in which we participate in Jesus Christ's offering to the Father on our behalf. Therefore, "It is Christ himself [...] who constitutes the living content, reality and power of the Eucharist" (ibid., 109). The Lord's Supper is an act of worship and thanksgiving, which takes place "within the circle of the life of Christ," as John McLeod Campbell would say. We are lifted up beyond our capacity to offer thanks to the Father in the vicarious offering of the life and death of Jesus Christ. We participate in His offering to the Father by partaking of His body and blood.

There is much more we could consider here, but this brief overview of Torrance's doctrine of the sacraments will suffice for a clearer understanding of Christ's vicarious humanity. We will move on from here to examine Torrance's usage of the Christological doctrines of *anhypostasis* and *enhypostasis,* which we will simply call the "an/en couplet."

AN/EN-HYPOSTASIS

The difficulties we often have in understanding the vicarious humanity of Christ all tend to revolve around the question of human agency and divine grace. What part do we have to play in salvation if Christ has done everything on our behalf? Are human beings simply removed from the equation, made passive objects without anything to offer? Is our relationship with God only a superficial one? What about the New Testament call for a personal response to God's grace?

There is a common deadlock in Christian theology between God's grace and the human response. We often assume that if God does everything, then human beings do nothing, or if human beings do something, then God does not do everything. This mindset considers the divine and human agencies *mutually exclusive*. How many theological arguments end between a "rock and a hard place," between the Calvinist perspective that God saves us sovereignly, or the Arminian perspective that we must choose God and respond to grace? Torrance's brilliant usage of the an/en couplet works to resolve this age-old dilemma.

We will take a step back and first define each term. The *enhypostasis* comprises of two parts: "en" and "hypostasis," meaning literally "in the person of the Son." This doctrine indicates that the humanity of Jesus is a genuine humanity within the person of the Son of God. The *anyhpostasis* includes "an" and "hypostasis," meaning "not a person" or "no personal being except in the Son." This doctrine indicates that the humanity of Jesus has no independent reality apart from the incarnation. There is only one person, the Son of God, who is at once fully God and fully human; but while the humanity of Jesus Christ is a real and true humanity, it has no independent existence apart from the incarnation. In other words, the humanity of Jesus is both fully *dependent* on the Son of God and a truly *genuine* humanity. This is the twofold consideration implied by the an/en couplet.

Together these two concepts simply mean that while Jesus' humanity would have no independent reality apart from the incarnation, that humanity is nevertheless fully real *in* the person of the Son of God. These are both rather technical terms for Christology, but they become important for discussing the role of divine grace and the human response in Torrance's thought.

Geordie W. Ziegler makes a helpful remark on how Torrance uses the an/en couplet:

> In Torrance's view, the an/en couplet opens up conceptual space for a dynamic way of describing divine and human agency in Christ that illuminates the key features of the motion of Grace, which Chalcedon's negative assertions fail to capture. While the person of

the Son remains the single hypostasis or agent of the God-human, the human Jesus is no mere instrument in the hand of God, but a full human person with human body, mind, reason, will and soul.

— TRINITARIAN GRACE AND PARTICIPATION, KINDLE
LOC. 2097-2106

The an/en couplet then allows "the divine will and the human will [to] coexist without confusion or separation" (ibid.). The humanity of Jesus is genuine, it is a humanity which has not been *overmastered* by the divinity of the Son of God, but neither is it a humanity *independent* of the Son. The an/en couplet gives space for both the humanity and divinity of Christ to operate without separation or confusion.

Torrance writes:

All through the incarnate life and activity of the Lord Jesus we are shown that 'all of grace' does not mean 'nothing of man', but precisely the opposite: *all of grace means all of man,* for the fulness of grace creatively includes the fullness and completeness of our human response in the equation. But this is not something that can be understood logically, for logically 'all of grace' would mean 'nothing of man', which may tempt people to apportion the role of Christ and of the believer by arguing for 'something of grace' and 'something of man', something done *for me* by Christ and something I do *for myself! All* of grace means *all* of man! We must remember that in all his healing and saving relations with us Jesus Christ is engaged in personalising and humanising (never depersonalising or dehumanising) activity, so that in all our relations with him we are made more truly and fully human in our personal response of faith than ever before. This takes place in us through the creative activity of the Holy Spirit as he unites us to the perfect humanity of the Lord

Jesus conceived by the Holy Spirit, born of the Virgin Mary and raised again from the dead.

— THE MEDIATION OF CHRIST, XII

Torrance uses the an/en-hypostasia to express that "all of grace means all of man," since there is at once a true humanity and true deity in the person of Jesus Christ. Just as the human nature of Jesus Christ was a real and genuine humanity, so our human responses in Him are real and genuine. However, we do not respond *independent* of Him, just as the humanity of Christ has no independent reality apart from the incarnation. This is how we must think if we are to move beyond the impasse between God's grace and the human response. It is "all of grace" *and* "all of man," although this cannot be logically conceived without a Christological basis in the an/en-hypostasia.

Torrance explains this further within the context of the sacraments:

The act of God in baptism is to be understood in terms of the reciprocity between divine and human *agency* which he has established for us in the whole historical Jesus Christ and which he continues to maintain with us in the space-time structures of our worldly existence through his Spirit [...] God unites us with Christ in such a way that his human agency in vicarious response to the Father overlaps with our response, gathers it up in its embrace, sanctifying, affirming and upholding it in himself, so that it is established in spite of all our frailty as our free and faithful response to the Father in him [...]

That is what holy baptism is about—we do not baptise ourselves but are baptised in the Name of the Father and of the Son and of the Holy Spirit. On the ground of what Christ has done for us and in accordance with his promise, we are presented before God as subjects of his saving activity, and are initiated into a mutual relation between the act of the Spirit and the response of faith. Faith arises as the gift of the Spirit, while it is through faith that we may continue to receive the Spirit, and it is in the Spirit that God continues to act creatively upon us, uniting us to Christ so that his atoning reconciliation bears fruit in us, and lifting us up to share in the very life and love of God, in the communion of the Father, the Son and the Holy Spirit. Baptism is thus not a sacrament of what we do but of what God has done for us in Jesus Christ, in whom he has bound himself to us and bound us to himself, before we could respond to him... baptism tells us that it is not our act of faith or on our own faithfulness that we rely, but upon Christ alone and his vicarious faithfulness

— THEOLOGY IN RECONCILIATION, 102-4

It is only *in* and *through* Christ's vicarious humanity that we personally respond to God, but we do genuinely respond. So while we are not puppets in God's hands, we are nevertheless wholly *dependent* on Jesus Christ and His vicarious response to the Father as we personally respond to God.

In a sense, we might say Jesus Christ *is* our objective relationship with God, who at once includes our subjective relationship, upholds it, perfects it, and yet retains its real and genuine humanity. We become more fully and truly human persons in our response to God already included in Christ's response. We are not stripped of our humanity. The an/en couplet holds together this tension. His vicarious response is the objective reality upholding our subjective response, and His objective response does not negate the genuineness of our response. Christ is the solid ground upon which we build our home, while our own self-justifying efforts are the house built on sand destined to crumble beneath us (Mt. 7:24-27).

You may be able to see why this is a helpful alternative to the former ways of thinking about grace and the human response. Instead of thinking in strict black-and-white, either-or terms, we think *Christologically,* placing Jesus Christ's vicarious humanity at the center of our understanding. *In Him*, we respond to the grace of the Father.

We are free to joyfully respond to the Father, through the Son, and in the Holy Spirit. We are not thrown back upon ourselves to worry about the adequacy of our response. We rely wholly on the humanity of Jesus Christ as our perfect vicarious response to the grace of God. We are neither excluded from responding to God's grace, nor are we left to work up an independent response on our own, but we participate in the vicarious humanity of Jesus Christ as He perfectly responds to the Father. We are at once *genuinely free* and *totally dependent* on Him.

SIDEBAR: FALLEN HUMANITY

There is a theological debate of no small importance related to Torrance's doctrine of the vicarious humanity of Christ. This is the debate regarding what sort of humanity God assumed in the incarnation. Was it merely a *neutral* humanity, or was it our *fallen* and *sinful* human nature that Christ took up as His own? For Torrance, it must be truly *our* humanity, or else Christ has not truly penetrated our darkness or reached us in our estrangement from God. And if God has not truly reached us as we are in our fallen, sinful state, then we cannot be re-created from the depths of our existence and reconciled to the Triune life of God. It must truly be *our* humanity that Jesus makes His own, or else salvation takes place "over our heads," without being properly grounded in our actual existence. Torrance therefore strongly affirms that God assumed a *fallen* human nature in Jesus Christ.

There is a careful distinction to be made here. When Torrance insists Christ assumed our *fallen* humanity as His own, this—of course—does not mean Christ Himself sinned. He remained sinless even in assuming our fallen nature. This is well in line with Paul's conclusion: "For our sake he made him to be sin who knew no sin, so that in him we might become the righteousness of God" (2 Cor. 5:21). Jesus Christ took up, as His own, our sinful humanity without *sinning* within our humanity; He became sin who knew no sin and lived a sinless life from within our fallen humanity. Torrance writes:

> [T]he Incarnation was the coming of God to save us in the heart of our *fallen* and *depraved* humanity, where humanity is at its wickedest in its enmity and violence against the reconciling love of God. That is to say, the Incarnation is to be understood as the coming of God to take upon himself our fallen human nature, our actual human existence laden with sin and guilt, our humanity diseased in mind and soul in its estrangement or alienation from the Creator [...] The whole man had to be assumed by Christ if the whole man was to be saved [...] the unassumed is unhealed [...] what God has not taken up in Christ is not saved.
>
> — The Mediation of Christ, 39

For Torrance, if Jesus did not truly take up *our humanity* in becoming a human, then He cannot truly be *our* savior. If He was not really one of us, our brother sharing in our fallen condition, then His humanity would be no more than a mask or an illusion. This would be a "Docetic" humanity, referring to the early heresy that Christ only "appeared" human. Torrance is strongly against such an understanding of Christ's humanity and insists Christ truly took up *our* corrupt existence as His own.

I am aware this notion may raise several problems for readers. I have no interest in defending Torrance's position, though I do think he is right. However, my main concern is simply to bring it to your attention. Whatever issues arise from this may be resolved by reading Torrance's work on the subject, although it is not a subject he treats exhaustively in any one book.

As an alternative, Daniel Cameron has written an excellent study on the debate, with a particular focus on Torrance. His book works well to answer many of the issues that naturally arise when considering the doctrine. Therefore, I would recommend reading Cameron's book, *Flesh and Blood,* before jumping to conclusions about this. I'd also suggest Myk Habets' book, *Theology in Transposition,* which includes a helpful chapter on the subject (chapter seven).

For now, we will conclude by simply stating that, for Torrance, this is a non-negotiable. If Jesus has not truly assumed *our* real (fallen) human nature, then He has not truly been *our* savior. This is an essential component in Torrance's doctrine of the vicarious humanity of Christ.

Accordingly, for Torrance, Christ's assumption of a fallen human nature is essential because it culminates in the sanctification of our human nature. Without a firm grasp of this doctrine, the Gospel lacks a proper understanding of objective sanctification in Christ. Torrance writes:

> If the incarnate Son through his birth of the Virgin Mary actually assumed our flesh of sin, the fallen, corrupt and enslaved human nature which we have all inherited from Adam, then the redeeming activity of Christ took place within the ontological depths of his humanity in such a way that far from sinning himself, he condemned sin in the flesh and sanctified what he assumed, so that incarnating and redeeming events were one and indivisible, from the very beginning of his earthly existence to its end in his death and resurrection.
>
> — "Incarnation and Atonement," 12; cited in Myk Habets: Theology in Transposition, 188

Torrance understands Christ's assumption of our fallen human nature as a saving and healing work. In the same way that Jesus healed the lepers and made the sick well by touching them, so He embraced our sinful humanity in order to heal us from within. If Christ did not assume our sinful human nature, then sin is not truly condemned in our flesh or sanctified by Him in its ontological depths. This is the importance of the doctrine for Torrance.

8

THREEFOLD ATONEMENT

SUMMARY: Torrance's doctrine of the atonement is multi-faceted. He outlines a "threefold" understanding of Christ's atoning death in the light of three Hebraic terms: *padah*, *kipper*, and *goel*. This threefold understanding does not exhaustively describe Torrance's complex doctrine of the atonement, but it is an aspect we will focus on here. Ultimately, Torrance insists that the doctrine of the atonement must remain *open-ended*. It cannot be closed in by fixating on a single "theory." The atonement is "more to be adored than expressed."

IN TORRANCE'S OWN WORDS:

The atoning death of Christ is to be approached with the greatest reverence and awe as holy mystery ultimately grounded in the infinite being of God. The reason for the atonement, its why and its how, is hidden in the holy love of God, before which the very angels veil their faces and which they shield from our prying minds.

— THE MEDIATION OF CHRIST, XIII

The cross is a window opened into the very heart of God.

— Ibid., 112

If I did not believe in the cross, I could not believe in God. The cross means that, while there is no explanation of evil, God himself has come into the midst of it in order to take it upon himself, to triumph over it, and deliver us from it.

— Preaching Christ Today, 29

Secondary quotes:

Torrance's soteriology [doctrine of salvation] is not readily put into a convenient category [...] In the end, perhaps, it would be wrong to suggest that Torrance has any theory of the atonement at all, for a theory was not what he was after. His is a soteriology a posteriori [after the fact], a confessional rather than an explanatory soteriology. I might be pushing this too far, but at times it reads as if it were a worship-full soteriology. It is theology as bearing witness to the essential mystery and miracle of God in Christ for us.

— Andrew Purves: Exploring Christology and
Atonement, 238

Introduction

In the previous chapter, we came to discover that, for Torrance, the incarnation is soteriological (saving) and the atonement is incarnational (rooted in the person of the mediator, Jesus Christ). While there are many healing and saving considerations in Torrance's work on the incarnation, the work of the atonement is not found only in the life of Jesus. Torrance still understands the culmination of Christ's saving work to be His death, resurrection, and ascension to the right hand of the Father.

In this chapter, we will briefly explore a "threefold" atonement model found in Torrance's thought. Three Hebraic terms root Torrance's thinking in the history and culture of Israel. We will focus on these and on how they are interconnected.

Torrance's doctrine of the atonement is one of the most complex areas of his theology. I am not attempting to study *every* aspect of Torrance's doctrine in this chapter but focus on the insights that have helped me the most. There are several considerations I have left out for the sake of space and clarity. Torrance's posthumous volume, *Atonement: The Person and Work of Christ,* is his most exhaustive treatment of the doctrine (though incomplete without its partner volume, *Incarnation*), and I recommend it for a more systematic study. By focusing on this aspect of Torrance's work, I do not mean to imply that this is the *only* thing he has to say about the atonement. In fact, it would likely take an entire book to survey Torrance's full contribution.

OVERVIEW

The three Hebraic terms that make up this "threefold" atonement are *goel, padah,* and *kipper* (sometimes transliterated *g'l, pdh,* and *kpr*). Torrance calls these the "ontological," "priestly," and "dramatic" forms of the atonement (see *The Trinitarian Faith,* 170-1). These terms are interconnected, with no single term being rightly considered without the others. They each clarify an essential aspect of the atonement. Instead of trying to fit the atonement into a presupposed theory, Torrance sees the interrelation of all three perspectives as essential to an understanding of the whole. Yet, ultimately, he understands that the atonement is a mystery beyond all human comprehension. Therefore, even in describing the atonement, we must recognize that our statements are open-ended, mere pointers to the reality they correspond to —a reality we can only approach with wonder and thanksgiving.

This naturally follows from Torrance's scientific thought, which stressed the need for a fundamental "openness" to the truth of reality (as we explored in chapter two). The atonement, then, is "more to be adored than expressed." These Hebraic terms are not to be understood as rigid dogmatic statements which *contain* the atonement, but perhaps we might see them best as *portals* through which we glimpse a small taste of the unfathomable riches of the cross. God's saving, reconciling, and redeeming work cannot be reduced to a mere theory, nor should it be. Torrance's work on the atonement remains *open* to its mystery rather than *closed* in by rigid statements. It will be important to keep this in mind as we describe these three terms.

PADAH OR "THE DRAMATIC"

Pdh with its cognates speaks of redemption as a mighty act of God bringing deliverance from oppression, as in the redemption of Israel out of Egypt and the house of bondage, and from the power of death. It refers very significantly to a redemption at once out of the oppression of evil and out of the judgement of God upon it, but with emphasis upon the cost of redemption through the substitutionary offering of a life for a life, and also upon the dramatic nature of the redeeming act as a sheer intervention on the part of God in human affairs. It is essentially an act of redemption from unlawful thraldom [slavery] which strips it of its vaunted right and usurped authority, bringing them to nothing, so that the impossible idea of a ransom being paid to evil does not and could not arise.

— THE TRINITARIAN FAITH, 170

The emphasis of this term falls on the *nature* of the atonement as a "dramatic" work of God's saving grace. The classic atonement theory known as *Christus Victor* is brought to mind here. With this, we recognize the nature of the atonement as God's mighty act of gracious redemption, in which we are delivered from the powers of sin and death in parallel with the deliverance of the Israelites from Egypt.

Summarizing *Christus Victor*, Gustaf Aulén, in his famous book on the subject, writes, "The work of Christ is first and foremost a victory over the powers which hold mankind in bondage: sin, death, and the devil" (*Christus Victor*, 20). Torrance takes issue with the notion of any ransom offered to the devil. But, generally speaking, this Hebraic term is reminiscent of the classical *Christus Victor* model, though it is not exclusively confined to it or equal with it. The focus, for Torrance, is the way this term was used in describing the redemption of Israel from out of Egypt. In a similar manner, Christ's cross was the redemption of sinners from the captivity of sin, death, and judgment.

Another similarity could be drawn here between Torrance's usage of *padah* and one of his primary Patristic teachers, St. Athanasius. In his famous work, *On the Incarnation*, Athanasius writes:

> Thus, taking a body like our own, because all our bodies were liable to the corruption of death, He surrendered His body to death instead of all, and offered it to the Father. This He did out of sheer love for us, so that in His death all might die, and the law of death thereby be abolished because, having fulfilled in His body that for which it was appointed, it was thereafter voided of its power for men. This He did that He might turn again to incorruption men who had turned back to corruption, and make them alive through death by the appropriation of His body and by the grace of His resurrection. Thus He would make death to disappear from them as utterly as straw from fire.
>
> — ON THE INCARNATION, §8

Padah is rightly called the "dramatic" aspect of the atonement, because, through the substitutionary offering of a life for a life, God's saving grace sets us free from the bondage of sin and death. Yet this freedom includes the destruction of sin and death itself. Sin and death are not merely stripped of their power but are made to "disappear [...] as utterly as straw from fire." That is, sin and death are *themselves* put to death in Christ's substitutionary death. Torrance notes this by considering the Greek word *luō*:

> It is through destroying the usurped power of the law and darkness over man that the redeemer 'leads captivity captive' and opens up an entirely new situation in which the old order is annulled and a new order of freedom in the Spirit is ushered in.
>
> To this conception of redemption the Greek language [...] offers its rich contribution, for *luō* means both to destroy and loosen, set free or liberate, that is, dissolution and absolution. Thus the Greek tends to strengthen the double significance of redemption as a destruction of the power of evil and also a liberation from evil, a loosing from sin and guilt, and so of forgiveness and cancellation of debt.
>
> — ATONEMENT, 32

The mighty act of God to overcome sin includes the destruction of sin together with the circumcision of our old sinful nature (Col. 2:11), just as it includes Christ's overcoming of death together with the promised final victory of life over death in the new creation (1 Cor. 15:26). Our old ways were put to death in Christ's death. Egypt is no longer an option for us like it was for the Israelites, because the old nature, Egypt itself, has been destroyed once and for all in Christ's death.

The dramatic element is the sheer graciousness of God to act in our place for our redemption. Christ conquers sin and the grave, putting death to death, substituting His life for ours. There is no trace of the old bondage of sin or death anymore. This deliverance is purely God's redeeming work, an act of God's powerful grace. We are set free, not by anything we have done but because God has made us free. Freedom from the powers of darkness through God's mighty act of redemption is what Torrance means by using the Hebraic term *padah*.

Torrance offers this summary:

Padah - Redemption by a mighty hand in sheer grace, at once out of the oppression of evil and out of judgement and death. But the mighty hand is the holiness of Christ, his obedience unto the death of the cross. The mighty hand is the blood of Christ, shed freely on our behalf. Here the stress is laid upon the nature of the redeeming act.

— ATONEMENT, 51

KIPPER OR "THE PRIESTLY"

Kpr with its cognates has to do with the expiatory form of the act of redemption, the sacrifice by which the barrier of sin and guilt between God and man is done away and propitiation is effected between them. This is primarily a cultic concept of redemption, but one in which God is always the subject and never the object of the reconciling or atoning act, for even when it is liturgically carried out through a priest, it is only by way of witness to the fact that it is God himself who by his own judicial and merciful act makes atonement and blots out sin. Atonement is here understood as involving both judgement upon the wrong through the offering of an equivalent, or of life for life, and restoration to favour and holiness before God.

— THE TRINITARIAN FAITH, 170-1

The emphasis of this term falls on the *means* or *mode* of the atonement as a "priestly" act of God's love. An important consideration, for Torrance, is recognizing that God was not the *object* of the atonement; God remained its *subject*. In simple terms, this means that God was the one who *acted* in the atonement and was not *acted upon*. The atonement was not a pagan offering to appease (act upon) an "angry God," in the sense that Christ's death caused a change *in God*. The opposite is true. While the death of Jesus Christ was truly offered up to the Father in the Holy Spirit, the *object* of the atonement was the sin and guilt of human beings. The change enacted on the cross was a change *in humanity*. God was in Christ blotting out the sin and guilt inherent to our fallen existence, putting to death the "old man" for the sake of the new, and reconciling the world to Himself (Heb. 8:12, 2 Cor. 5:14-21). God was the acting subject of the atonement, not the object acted upon.

So while this Hebraic term is reminiscent of an atonement theory known as "penal substitution," it is at once drastically different from many of the common interpretations of it. Torrance might reject penal substitution in the sense that it often makes God the object of the atonement. (For this and other modern critiques of penal substitution, see Belousek's excellent book, *Atonement, Justice, and Peace*.) Torrance does, however, affirm "expiation" in the atonement, in the sense that God's Triune act in Jesus Christ put an end to sin by offering up the death of the Son to the Father—not to appease the Father but to over-come sin and guilt. Thus, Torrance clarifies the term "propitiation," which has often been wrongly used to mean *appeasement*:

> By 'propitiation', of course, is not meant any placating or conciliation [appeasement] of God on our part, for God is never acted upon by means of priestly sacrifice offered by human beings. Thus as in the Old Testament liturgy it is always God himself who provides the sacrifice whereby he draws near to the worshipper and draws the worshipper near to himself, so in the actualised liturgy of the life, death, resurrection and ascension of Jesus Christ, it is God himself who in atoning propitiation draws near to us and draws us near to himself. God does not love us, Calvin once wrote, because he has reconciled us to himself; it is because he loved us that he has reconciled us to himself.
>
> — THE MEDIATION OF CHRIST, 110

The cross was an *overflow* of God's love, not the *reason* for God's love. Far too often the atonement is painted with violent words as if

God's wrath and judgment were the central themes of the whole event. Yet it was not the wrath of God that motivated the atonement but God's unwavering love for humanity even in the face of our sin and corruption. The crucifixion was no dark day, which is why we call it "Good Friday" and not "bad Friday." God's love for us shined most clearly in Christ's death.

Notions of the atonement acting on God rather than God acting for us are alien both to the New Testament *and* the Old. Torrance explains further how this term was used in the Old Testament:

> The words for atonement, reconciliation, expiation, etc, are *not* used of action upon God, of placating God or propitiating him. God is not the object of this action, He is always subject. It is God himself who performs the act of forgiveness and atonement or expiation. The sacrifices are liturgical expiations which do not act upon God but answer to God's action in forgiveness and merciful cleansing of sin. Atoning sacrifices were sacrifices expiating sin in *witness* to the act of God.
>
> — ATONEMENT, 19

God's forgiveness was not the *result* of the sacrifices performed in the Old Testament but rather these sacrifices bore *witness* to God's forgiveness and mercy. We have often reversed the order and, as a result, interpreted Christ's death as enacting a change in God rather than in humanity. When we understand that the Old Testament liturgy was not the *cause* of God's mercy but rather its *witness,* then we will also recognize that Christ's death did not *cause* God to be merciful. Instead, the cross was the *overflow* of God's love. The cross *revealed* God's kindness towards us, it did not *cause* God to forgive us. God loves us and wills to be gracious and merciful towards us, and *therefore,* Christ died to blot out sin and put to death the sinner. Rightly understanding *kipper* in its Old Testament usage is crucial for understanding Torrance's work on the atonement.

Many of the recent criticisms of penal substitution hit the mark in showing how the doctrine fails to grasp the unity of the Father and Son in both being and act on the cross. If the cross is understood in terms of *causing* God's mercy, then the Son is a pagan sacrifice to appease God's wrath. This, first of all, misunderstands the original usage of *kipper* in the Old Testament, but it also ignores the oneness in being and act of the Father, Son, and Holy Spirit on the cross. Thus, Torrance writes of the mutual sacrifice of the Father, Son, and Holy Spirit:

> The fact that Jesus Christ is God's beloved Son means that in him the Father was actively and personally present in the crucifixion of Christ, intervening redemptively in our lostness and darkness. In giving his beloved Son in atoning sacrifice for our sin God has given himself to us in unreserved love, so that the cross is not only a revelation of the love of Christ but a revelation of the love of God. The cross was a window into the very heart of God, for in and behind the cross, it was God the Father himself who paid the cost of our salvation. And so through the shedding of the blood of Christ in atoning sacrifice for our sin the innermost nature of God the Father as holy compassionate love has been revealed to us.
>
> — IBID., 109

The death of Jesus Christ was a *priestly* act of substitution, not a pagan offering to appease God's anger by sacrifice. It was a Triune movement of grace and love to remove the sin and guilt of human beings, carrying both "outside the camp." Sin was taken away in Christ's death, death was put to death, and evil was robbed of its power. In Israel's priesthood, this was precisely what the sacrificial lamb was for, not a sacrifice to appease God's anger but a *substitute* to carry away the sins of the community. These sacrifices bore *witness* to God's mercy; they did not *cause* God's mercy. The substitution of a life for a life, the divine exchange, is important to keep in mind. Jesus

Christ suffered the death of a sinner in order to overcome both sin and death, forever blotting out its mark against us.

Central to expiation is the fact that God covers our sin, invalidating it, and placing it behind His back where it may no longer exist. This was the goal of Christ's priestly death unto God, not appeasement but expiation. The object was not God but sin. Sin, for Torrance, is a breach of the covenant that results in the threat of nonbeing. It was against *this* breach in the covenant, against sin, that the wrath of God was directed towards (and not necessarily human beings). As Torrance writes, "[T]he wrath of God is God's holiness and faithfulness directed against breaches in the covenant, and it is wrath *precisely because* God in his love affirms Israel to be his child and gives himself in covenant mercy to be Israel's God." (*Atonement,* 38; emphasis mine).

It is *because* God loves us that God's wrath was poured out against sin, destroying and overcoming it in Christ's death. Wrath is not an arbitrary threat. God's wrath is *purposeful.* It is a wrath *included* in God's love for us. God's wrath, in this sense, is the wrath *of* love, in a similar way that a loving parent might react quite fiercely against an attacker who seeks to harm their child. God's love is *for us,* and therefore, God's wrath is also a wrath *for us* and not against us. As the wrath of His love, God's wrath stands against that which stands against us, against the sin that seeks to destroy us. Therefore, a breach of the covenant must be overcome by the expiation of sin and guilt, and this is what Christ accomplished in His death and resurrection.

For this Torrance follows Barth's notion of the "Judge judged in our place" from *Church Dogmatics* IV/1. This is a kind of "ontological" substitutionary atonement, in which the Judge who judges sin suffers its judgment. Jesus Christ is at once the Judge and the One judged in our place. Torrance writes:

> He bears his own [divine] judgement of man in the flesh and in his own human existence [...] The agony of Jesus—and how he was constrained until it was accomplished—was that he was the judging God and the judged man at the same time, the electing God and the

elected man at the same time, and in this unspeakable tension he remained absolutely faithful as the Son of God and Son of Man.

— INCARNATION, 113

The priestly offering of the Son in His substitutionary death for us is what Torrance means with the term *kipper*.

Torrance offers this summary:

Kipper - Redemption by an expiatory sacrifice for sin made in the offering of Christ's life for our life in obedience to the divine will and mercy. He is both the priest and the sacrifice in one, lamb-and-servant of God, shedding his blood in costly ransom or expiation, in order to remove the barrier of guilt and enmity between man and God and God and man and so effect reconciliation in a holy communion between them. Here the stress is upon the mode of the atoning redemption and on the restoration to fellowship with God that it effects.

— ATONEMENT, 52

GOEL OR "THE ONTOLOGICAL"

G'l with its cognates refers to a concept of redemption out of destitution or bondage or forfeited rights undertaken by the advocacy of someone who is related to the person in need through kinship or some other bond of affinity or covenant love. In this type of redemption the focus is on the nature of the redeemer, the person of the *go'el*, who claims the cause of the one in need as his own, and stands in for him since he cannot redeem himself. In the Old Testament this remarkable conception of redemption is also applied to God who acts on Israel's behalf in virtue of his special relation with Israel through election and covenant. It is on the ground of this bond and because of the blood of the covenant forging it that God takes the cause of his people upon himself as their kinsman-advocate, justifying them in the face of accusation and making sure their redemption in himself, and thus delivers them out of bondage into the freedom of their inheritance in communion with himself.

— The Trinitarian Faith, 171

The emphasis of this term falls on the nature of the *Redeemer,* whose very "being" acts for us in the atonement. Thus, Torrance calls it the "ontological" element. God has taken up our cause as His own in the person and work of Jesus Christ. We are not alone in our darkness or our sin; we are not left by ourselves to save ourselves. Jesus Christ became our brother, true flesh of our flesh and bone of our bone, to lead us back to His Father. It is the *kinship* of Jesus, His sheer humanity, that is emphasized with this term. In the history of Israel, this is the co-suffering of God, God's *pathos,* as we see in Jeremiah 50:34, "Their Redeemer is strong; the Lord of hosts is his name. He will surely plead their cause" (ESV). God is our advocate. God pleads our cause and acts on our behalf.

Torrance often quoted Gregory of Nazianzus, who said, "The unassumed is the unhealed." The converse of this means that whatever Christ has assumed He has healed. If Christ truly assumed our fallen humanity, He brought healing to our diseased existence. God did not come *in* the form of a human being, but God truly came *as* a human. This involves God's personal activity from within our humanity as our brother, as a fellow human being. Of course, Jesus Christ is at once God, which is why His being one with us is so significant. If Jesus was only a human, then He could not save us, because no human can break free from the limitations of their humanity. If Jesus was only God, then God has not truly *reached us.* Whatever salvation God might provide in this scenario would be transactional, not ontological, having to do with a salvation over our heads with no grounding in our actual existence. But since God has come as a human, fully God and fully human, then Jesus Christ has truly *reached us* in our dark-

ness. He has *lifted us* out of our estrangement into fellowship
with God.

This aspect of the atonement also emphasizes the fact that we are
not merely saved *from* something, be it sin or death. Although it is true
we are saved from these things, the greater truth of the Gospel is that
we are saved *for God.* Through the Holy Spirit and in union with
Christ we are lifted up into fellowship with the Triune love of God.
This is often missing in our presentations of the Gospel, but in emphasizing the *goel* aspect of the atonement, Torrance regains an apprecia-
tion of the Gospel as a message of *reconciliation* (not merely of
escaping hell). We will have more to say about this in the next chapter,
but Torrance himself notes this in the context of sanctification:

> But because it is God who acts as *goel,* his redemption is at once
> judging and saving. Not only does he redeem us out of bondage and
> death, but he draws us into his holiness and sanctifies us with it, so
> that in redemption we are given to share in the sanctification of
> the Lord.
>
> — ATONEMENT, 47

The incarnation and atoning death of Jesus Christ causes an "ontological" change in our very being. In wonderfully colorful language,
Torrance writes:

> By pouring forth upon men unconditional love, by extending freely
> to all without exception total forgiveness, by accepting men purely on
> the ground of the divine grace, Jesus became the centre of a volcanic
> disturbance in human existence, for He not only claimed the whole
> of man's existence for God but exposed the hollowness of the
> foundations upon which man tries to establish himself before God.
>
> — GOD AND RATIONALITY, 66

What if we thought more of Christ's life as a "volcanic distur-
bance" in human existence and less as merely a means to an end? This
would result in an important rethinking of our doctrine of the atonement, in which the kinship Christ shares with us involves a fundamental change in our nature. The ontological change in humanity
through the incarnation and atoning death of Christ *as* a human is
what Torrance means by the term *goel.*

Torrance offers this summary:

> *Goel* - Redemption by a kinsman-advocate, who acting out of a
> blood tie or covenant bond, or who out of pure love forging such a
> bond in himself and in the blood of the new covenant, stands in our
> place, takes our lost cause on himself as his own, makes sure our
> redemption in himself, and so delivers us out of our bondage into
> the freedom of our inheritance in God. Here the stress is upon the
> nature of the redeemer and our kinship with him.
>
> — ATONEMENT, 52

THE UNITY OF THE THREE

Torrance admits these three terms are not so evenly separated in
the scriptures. Likewise, in discussing the work of Athanasius,
Torrance remarked how "the dramatic, the priestly and the ontological,
were never separated but were held together" (*The Trinitarian Faith,*
175). The same is true for Torrance's usage of each term. All three
aspects must be thought through together, and no one concept
completes the whole picture apart from the others. There is also no
unequal emphasis on one concept over the others, as all three have
essential roles to play in the atonement. Thus, Torrance writes:

> [N]one of these aspects can stand alone or become the major basis of
> a doctrine of atonement, without serious dislocation of the biblical

understanding and failure to appreciate the fullness of Christ's saving
work.

— ATONEMENT, 53

We will follow Torrance's explanation for why each term cannot be
rightly understood without the others, as well as his exploration of
what happens when each term is isolated. (I have added parentheses to
clarify which term is meant since only numbers were used in the original. Direct quotations are from Torrance; everything else is my own
summary.)

The dramatic element (*padah*, 1) without the priestly element (*kipper*,
2) results in "an ultimate dualism" (*Atonement*, 53), such as the notion
of a ransom paid to the devil. Without the ontological element (*goel*,
3), the dramatic element (*padah*, 1) is "dissolved into mere events"
(ibid.). That is, without a grounding in the historical reality of Jesus
Christ it becomes a timeless mystery. This results in an existentializa-
tion or subjectivization (an existential or subjective reduction) of the
Gospel into a private event with no actual correspondence to Jesus
Christ. The dramatic therefore needs both the priestly and the ontological aspects.

The priestly element (*kipper*, 2) apart from the dramatic element
(*padah*, 1) "degenerates into a pagan notion of placating God" (ibid.).
Without the emphasis of a sheer act of grace intervening in our
humanity, "[I]t becomes a Pelagian, sacerdotalist conception of
appeasing an angry God through human mediation" (ibid., 54). The
priestly element (*kipper*, 2) without the ontological element (*goel*, 3)
"degenerates into a legal and cultic fiction with no basis in actual existence and reality and therefore with no relevance to our actual humanity. Thus the doctrine of justification apart from union with Christ
cannot avoid the charge of a legal fiction. Moreover, failing to take

(*goel*, 3) seriously would mean a failure to see the saving significance of the humanity of Jesus Christ. Apart from both (*padah*, 1) and (*goel*, 3) the proper doctrine of Christ as himself the only mediator and our high priest would disappear, and then (*padah*, 2) would degenerate into ritualistic superstition" (ibid.). The priestly therefore needs both the dramatic and the ontological aspects.

The ontological element (*goel*, 3) apart from the dramatic element (*padah*, 1) would result in an adoptionist Christology, in which redemption is brought about through a kind of "moral influence" where Jesus Christ "becomes" god-like rather than Himself God in sheer grace as a human. The ontological element (*goel*, 3) apart from the priestly (*kipper*, 2) "would degenerate into a doctrine of deification through union with deity" therefore turning into "sheer idealism" (ibid.). Apart from (*padah*, 1) and (*kipper*, 2), "stress upon (*goel*, 3) would result in a conception of redemption through mystic absorption into the divine" (ibid.). The ontological therefore needs both the dramatic and priestly aspects.

We might refer to these terms as a threefold cord. Any unequal emphasis on one concept over the others results in a disruption of the whole. Many errors in the doctrine of the atonement come from a wrongful emphasis on one of these aspects apart from the others. Torrance has brilliantly stressed the threefold nature of Christ's atoning life and death as at once dramatic (*padah*), priestly (*kipper*), and ontological (*goel*). All three taken together form a solid basis for any sound doctrine of the atonement.

Summing everything up, Torrance makes a helpful comparison between these three terms and the "threefold office" of Christ:

(1) Padah redemption - kingly office of Christ - active obedience.

(2) Kipper redemption - priestly office of Christ - passive obedience.

(3) Goel redemption - prophetic office of Christ - incarnational assumption of our humanity.

— ATONEMENT, 60

INCARNATIONAL ATONEMENT

Perhaps Torrance's greatest contribution to the doctrine of the atonement is his dedication to an incarnational framework, which grounds the atonement firmly in the person of Jesus Christ. Elmer Colyer writes:

> Torrance sees the New Testament understanding of redemption developed in light of Jesus' own self-interpretation through an appropriation of the three Hebrew terms associated with redemption in the Old Testament—pdh, kpr and g'l—as well as their cognates... Torrance develops his realist and holistic doctrine of the atonement by drawing together these three aspects (the dramatic or dynamic, the priestly or cultic, and the ontological), with the ontological (incarnational) providing the overall pattern.

— HOW TO READ T.F. TORRANCE, 90

An incarnational framework is the overarching structure behind Torrance's doctrine of the atonement. This is the natural conclusion of Torrance's insistence that the atonement is to be known in the light of the incarnation. It is also the outworking of Torrance's conviction that person and work are never separated. As such, the atonement is best understood in the light of the incarnate life of the Son of God, and our doctrine of the atonement, therefore, must be placed within an incarnational framework. Only by thinking in the light of the incarnation will we properly understand the atonement.

Torrance wrote an important essay on the atoning obedience of Christ that highlights this point quite well (first published in the 1959

Moravian Theological Seminary Bulletin). Torrance begins: "Any adequate account of the atoning life and work of Christ must consider it from two aspects, the life and faithfulness of the Incarnate Son toward men, and the life and faithfulness of the Incarnate Son toward the Father" ("The Atoning Obedience of Christ," 65). Torrance clearly has in mind the Godward and humanward agency of Christ, but he is drawing out the atoning effect of Christ's faithfulness lived as both God and a human being. Notice how he does not merely say Christ's atoning *work* but makes a point to talk about Christ's "atoning *life* and work" (emphasis mine).

Torrance explores this within the context of prayer. Understood in the larger context of Christ's reconciling life and work, Christ's *entire* life takes on a new relevance for the doctrine of the atonement. The act of prayer itself becomes an "essentially redemptive activity" (ibid., 68). From within the poverty of our fallen humanity, Jesus Christ lived a life of faithful obedience to the Father, enacting a reconciled humanity from within our flesh. Torrance writes:

> It is in our place that Jesus prays, standing where we stand in our rebellion and alienation, existing where we exist in our refusal of divine grace and in our will to be independent, to live our own life in self-reliance. In that condition Jesus prays against the whole trend of our existence and against the whole self-willed movement of our life, for when Jesus prays it means that He casts Himself in utter reliance upon God the Father, in utter dependence upon His will, and refuses to draw a single breath except in that reliance and dependence. In this Jesus prays as a creature fulfilling the covenant prayer of creation to the Father, but He prays it from within our alienation and in battle against our self-will.
>
> — IBID., 69

This is an excellent example of the incarnational framework of the doctrine of atonement. The prayers Jesus prayed in our fallen humanity were acts of atoning reconciliation. He fought back against our fallen humanity and overcame our sinful nature through a perfect and faithful communion with the Father in the Spirit. Through His incarnate life we are reconciled to God; through His prayers within our fallen humanity, we pray "in Jesus name" before the Father. This is why Torrance says, "The embodiment of that relation of the Son to the Father in a perfect human life on earth was therefore, a fact of volcanic significance for salvation and judgement, for revelation and reconciliation" (ibid., 81). While the Western Church tends to neglect Christ's life in its understanding of the atonement, Torrance rightly reminds us of its essential significance.

More adored than expressed

Torrance's "threefold" doctrine of the atonement is an important movement towards a more nuanced understanding of Christ's person and work for us, one that moves beyond reducing the cross down to a so-called "atonement theory." Torrance's doctrine is ultimately *open* towards the beauty of the atonement and does not attempt to *control* the atonement with a theory. Ziegler writes:

> Within Torrance's theology, these atonement metaphors are not to be viewed as strict categories or parts or divisions, but more like portals or entry points which reveal the same truth of salvation from a particular angle. Each overlaps with the others and defies strict schematization.
>
> — Trinitarian Grace and Participation, Kindle Loc. 2247

In discussing the doctrine of the Trinity, I noted that, for Torrance, the Holy Trinity is "more to be adored than expressed." We may use this same phrase to describe the way Torrance carefully navigates *describing* the atonement without *containing* or *controlling* it. Torrance has no "theory" for the atonement, in the strict sense of the word, but only attempts to describe the indescribable act of God in Christ for our reconciliation. A doctrine of the atonement must recognize that the reality we are discussing is far greater than the statements (or theories) we use to describe it. We must see the work of Jesus Christ in His atoning life and death as "more to be adored than expressed."

May we pause with awe and wonder at the mystery of salvation, and may we resist the temptation of *reducing* the glorious atoning work of Christ down to a series of simple, rationalized theories. Torrance warns about the reductionistic tendency of "atonement theories" on the first pages of his book, *Atonement*:

> We cannot have any mere theory of atonement. No merely theoretical understanding is possible, for abstract theoretic understanding does away with the essential mystery by insisting on the continuity of merely rational explanation.
>
> — ATONEMENT, 4

Rational understanding is necessary, but we should not misuse our intellect. This does not mean that the Gospel is nonsensical, or that we should not seek to refine our knowledge of the atonement. It does mean, however, that we must accept the limitations of our knowledge. The atonement is a mystery we may be able to describe to some extent, but we will never fully comprehend it. We may apprehend a measure of its reality, but we will never be able to construct a self-contained doctrine of the atonement, in which all things are clearly mapped out and all mysteries are resolved. We must remember it is a reality "more to be adored than expressed."

SIDEBAR: UNIVERSALISM AND LIMITED ATONEMENT

For Torrance, both the doctrines of limited atonement *and* universalism are dual heresies deriving from the same kind of problematic logic. They both rely on what Torrance calls a "logical-causal" relation between the death of Jesus Christ and the extent of salvation. This logic runs as follows: if Jesus died for all, then everyone is saved, but if only the elect are saved, then the atonement is limited. Torrance considers this to be a logical construction we cannot rely upon without falling into serious error. A "logical-causal" relation is a connection *we* assume must be true, but it ultimately oversteps its bounds by claiming to know what only God knows.

Torrance offered a clear definition of this "logical-causal" connection when he wrote about those who falsely claimed Karl Barth was a Universalist:

> Behind the charge of universalism against Barth there lies a controlling frame of thought which operates with a notion of external logico-causal connections. If Christ died for all men, then, it is argued, all men must be saved, whether they believe or not; but if all men are not saved, and some, as seems very

evident, do go to hell, then Christ did not die for all men. Behind both of these alternatives, however, there are two very serious mistakes.

— DIVINE INTERPRETATION, 64

Torrance thinks this is the direct result of what he calls the "Latin heresy":

> Let me repeat, the problem of universalism versus limited atonement is itself a manifestation of the 'latin heresy' at work within Protestant and Evangelical thought. If Karl Barth is still misunderstood or criticised over his approach to the efficacious nature and range of redemption, it must be through mistaken opposition to his faithfulness in thinking out as far as possible the implications of the oneness of the Person and Work of Christ, or of the inseparability of the incarnation and atonement.

— IBID., 65-6

Those who still operate with a form of the Latin heresy in their thinking (which by thinking external-relationally separates the incarnation from the atonement) build a logical-causal relation between the extent of the atonement necessitating either universalism or limited atonement. Torrance explains further:

> It is a logico-causalism of this kind, with Augustinian-Thomist, Protestant scholastics and Newtonian roots, that appears to supply the deterministic paradigm within which there arise the twin errors of limited atonement and universalism both of which, although in different ways, are rationalistic

constructions of the saving act of God incarnate in the life, death and resurrection of the Lord Jesus Christ.

— IBID., 65

The important point Torrance makes is that the Western tendency to "externalize" the inner workings of the Gospel creates a *rationalistic construction* out of the atonement. Here we mistakenly inject our own logic into the grace of God, attempting to interpret God's works not according to God but according to ourselves. This is, in a sense, our human attempt to control the atonement by reducing it to logical connections we can understand. Or, in other words, by creating a doctrine of atonement in our own image.

We imagine that A + B *must* = C, and, if we assume C is true, then B re-interprets the nature of A.

In this case, "A" is the atonement, and "C" is the dual heresy of either limited atonement or universalism. This makes "B" the logical connection *we* add to God's grace, which is, in fact, foreign to it. There is no logical = between A and C. In fact, while we may know A to some extent, we cannot know C. Only God knows the end, who is saved and who is not. By injecting B into the equation we wrongfully assume that *we* have all the facts at our disposal and therefore that *we* can balance the equation. But we must remember that the atonement is not under our logical control, it is God's free work of grace. We wrongfully add human-centric logic to God's grace, morphing it into a monstrosity of logical deductions that limit God's freedom when we place grace at the disposal of human logic. This ultimately results in the twin heresies of limited atonement and universalism. This, Torrance brilliantly deduces, is the crucial, rationalistic error both here-sies make. They are both deterministic systems, one that presupposes a system in which all are saved and the other in which God predeter-mines a limited number of individuals to be saved. Both collapse into allegiance for a *system* rather than to the love of God for lost sinners.

In an essay on universalism, Torrance stressed the sheer *irrationality* of sin and called it a "dogmatic fallacy" to rationalize sin or attempt to make it fit within a system of human logic ("Universalism or Election?", 313). But we cannot rationalize the illogical. This is true both for those who proclaim dogmatic universalism as a fact but *also* for those who claim dogmatic particularism (that some will definitely *not* be saved in the end). Torrance maintains an important tension with this. We must say that Christ died for all humanity, that God's grace extends to all, and that the atonement is complete and efficacious. We cannot, however, say *why* some are (perhaps) not saved in the end. Only God knows and can say these things, and we overstep our bounds by attempting to systematize a mystery or make logical the irrationality of sin. Thus, Torrance writes:

> It is because atoning reconciliation falls within the incarnate constitution of Christ's Person as Mediator, that it is atoning reconciliation which embraces all mankind and is freely available to all in the unconditional grace of God's Self-giving. Why some people believe and why others do not believe we cannot explain, any more than we can explain why evil came into the world. The Gospel does not offer us a logical or causal explanation of the origin or presence of evil, or of precisely how it is vanquished in the Cross of Christ. But it does tell us what the Lord God has done to deal with evil. It tells us that in his unlimited love God himself, incarnate in Jesus Christ, has entered into the dark and fearful depths of our depraved and lost existence subjected to death and judgement, in order to make our sin and guilt, our wickedness and shame, our misery and fate, our godlessness and violence, his own, thereby substituting himself for us, and making atonement for sin, so that he might redeem us from our alienation and restore us to fellowship with the Father, the Son and the Holy Spirit. The saving act of God in the blood of Christ is an unfathomable mystery before which the angels veil their faces and into which

we dare not and cannot intrude, but before which our minds
bow in wonder, worship and praise.

— DIVINE INTERPRETATION, 66

Western Christianity has a tremendously low tolerance for mystery,
and this is perhaps the reason we often run into the issue of reduction-
ism. I appreciate the way Torrance reminds us, in the midst of our
reductionistic tendencies, that our primary role is to stand in awe and
wonder before Christ's work of atonement. It is not a work we can
master or logically control—even though our "atonement theories"
make it sound like we do exactly that. The atonement is that which,
above all else, we must praise God for.

This inadvertently raises the question of assurance. With this in
mind Torrance concludes by highlighting the *certainty* we have even in
the midst of mystery:

> However, of this we can be perfectly certain: the blood of
> Christ, the incarnate Son of God who is perfectly and
> inseparably one in being and act with God the Father, means
> that God will never act toward any one in mercy and
> judgement at any time or in any other way than he has already
> acted in the Lord Jesus. There is no God behind the back of
> Jesus Christ, and no God but he who has shown us his face in
> the face of Jesus Christ, for Jesus Christ and the Father are one.
> What the Father is and does, Jesus Christ is and does; what
> Jesus Christ is and does the Father is and does.

— IBID.

While it is improper to make a logical leap to either universalism
or limited atonement from the death of Jesus Christ, this does not
mean we are without certainty in the grace of God. Any attempt to fit
the saving life and work of Christ into *our* preconceived system is a

wrongful attempt to master God, and Torrance argues this is precisely what we cannot do. There are just some things beyond the scope of what we can know in this life. Universalism and limited atonement, even if they are true, are both beyond what we can know without trespassing on what God alone knows.

We must remain faithful to the witness of scripture, and not overstep our bounds by attempting to make logical connections out of what is fundamentally a mystery. Jesus Christ died for all humanity and the atonement is efficacious, but we cannot say why some are saved and others are not, nor do we know the outcome of human history. Therefore, Torrance rejects both limited atonement and universalism.

WITH JESUS BESIDES GOD (UNION AND PARTICIPATION)

SUMMARY: The goal of the Gospel, for Torrance, is not the atonement alone. It is union with Christ and participation in the Triune life of God that makes up the ultimate goal of God's saving acts. The Gospel does not primarily proclaim salvation away *from* something but rather salvation *for the sake of* union with Christ and participation in the life of God (*theosis*). Therefore, the capstone of Torrance's theology is the resurrection and ascension of Jesus Christ; we are "with Jesus besides God" in the life and love of the Holy Trinity.

IN TORRANCE'S OWN WORDS:

Yet it is not atonement that constitutes the goal and end of that integrated movement of reconciliation but union with God in and through Jesus Christ in whom our human nature is not only saved, healed and renewed but lifted up to participate in the very light, life and love of the Holy Trinity.

— THE MEDIATION OF CHRIST, 66

With the birth and resurrection of Jesus, with Jesus himself, the relation of the world to God has been drastically altered, for everything has been placed on an entirely new basis, the unconditional grace of God.

— SPACE, TIME AND RESURRECTION, 34

As in the incarnation we have to think of God the Son becoming man without ceasing to be transcendent God, so in his ascension we have to think of Christ as ascending above all space and time without ceasing to be man or without any diminishment of his physical, historical existence.

— IBID., 129

SECONDARY QUOTES:

It is not yet salvation that our sins are forgiven. We must be restored to communion with the Father, and through Christ, in union with him, to enter into the life of the Holy Trinity itself.

— ANDREW PURVES: EXPLORING CHRISTOLOGY AND
ATONEMENT, 100

INTRODUCTION

The Gospel, for Torrance, is not *primarily* a message of how we can escape hell, find justification, or find forgiveness. Of course, these play a part in what makes the Gospel good news. However, there is a much more essential element to the Gospel. This is the stunning news that we are united to Jesus Christ and through Him participate in the Triune life and love of God. It is why Jesus became a human and died, why the Father gave His Son for us, and why the Holy Spirit has been sent to the Church. It was not merely to avoid hell or put us "in the black" on a legal ledger, but to be united with Christ and through Him to participate in God's Triune life. The Gospel does not only save us *from* sin and hell but, most of all, it brings us *into* the communion of the Triune God.

THE GOAL OF ATONEMENT

Western theology tends to reduce the Gospel to salvation *from sin*; but, for Torrance, it is not *what* God has saved us *from* that matters most, it is *who* Jesus saves us *for*. Union and communion with the Triune God is the ultimate goal of salvation. Torrance writes:

> This is the mighty act of the incarnation which is at once the act of God's humiliation and the act of man's exaltation, for he who in such amazing grace descended to make our lost cause his own, ascended *in accomplishment of his task*, elevating man into union and communion with the life of God.
>
> — INCARNATION, 57; EMPHASIS MINE

The Gospel is not good news of escape but of rescue, of returning home to the Father's embrace. We do not merely find freedom from sin and the sting of death in Christ, but we find ourselves included in a life of love and fellowship like no other, the Triune life and love of the Father, Son, and Holy Spirit. That which we are saved *from* matters, of course, but the divine fellowship we are saved *for* is far, far more significant. The emphasis must fall on our being saved *into a new life with God,* not merely *from sin.*

For Torrance, Jesus Christ Himself *is* the good news. It is not merely about what happened in the life and death of Jesus, but it is who Jesus is and was that constitutes the Gospel message. "Jesus not only announces the kingdom but is himself the good news" (*Incarnation*, 20). It is not merely a benefit from Jesus Christ we receive when accepting the good news, but primarily it is Jesus Himself who *is* the benefit of the Gospel. In union with Him, we share in all His benefits. We are justified, sanctified, healed, reconciled, and redeemed—but most of all we are included and participate in the Triune love of God.

The "decision" the Gospel calls us to consider is therefore not our own decision about God, but it is God's decision about us, since it is Jesus Christ who has joined Himself to us in the incarnation. When Torrance talks about union with God as the goal of the Gospel, he is not discussing anything that *we* decide to achieve in ourselves; this is the decision God has made for us. Our decision is then appropriated to His decision, as Torrance writes:

> The gospel announces to me that in Jesus Christ God has already taken a decision about me; it announces that my existence has already been invaded and brought under the sovereign rule of God's grace in the life, death, and resurrection of Christ; it announces that the kingdom of God has overtaken me in Christ, and that my destiny has been laid hold of by Christ and determined by his crucifixion. Therefore the gospel challenges me to appropriate the decision which God has already made about me in Christ; it challenges me to cast my lot in with Christ and share in the history of Christ who has given himself in sacrifice to be my saviour [...]
>
> I am [not] saved by my own act of faith or decision, according to the New Testament gospel what saves me is the obedience of Christ upon which I am summoned to cast all my reliance, for it is his obedience which saves me and it is Christ through his Spirit who gives me to share in his obedience. Thus my decision rests upon his decision for me: my faith is my reliance upon his faithfulness and a sharing in his faith.
>
> — INCARNATION, 26-8

While Torrance does not directly use the terms union or participation in this quotation, it is clear that the very heart of the Gospel proclamation centers on our being united in the Holy Spirit to Jesus

Christ and in union with Him participating in His vicarious life for us. In this example, the decision which we are called to is not our own but Christ's, yet we still decide ourselves by appropriating His decision for us.

Therefore, it is not only the *goal* of salvation that we are united to Jesus Christ and participate in the Triune life of God, but union with Christ is also the *means* of our salvation. It is only through Him and in the Holy Spirit that we enjoy the benefits of salvation such as forgiveness, justification, and sanctification. The order is often reversed as if we work ourselves up into union with Christ, but Torrance thinks union with Christ is such an essential element to salvation that every aspect of the Gospel is permeated with it.

Torrance emphasized this when discussing the atonement in the light of the resurrection, writing, "Resurrection is atonement in its creative and positive result and achievement, in the recreation and final affirmation of man and the assuming of him by grace into union and communion with the life and love of God himself" (*Space, Time and Resurrection*, 56).

In a similar way that John McLeod Campbell emphasized the need for both a "downwards" atonement and an "upwards" atonement (or a negative and a positive atonement, "from" sin and "to" God), so Torrance understands union and communion with God as the *goal* of the atonement, as the positive to the negative of Christ's death. Andrew Purves summarizes McLeod Campbell: "Salvation is understood in terms of our participation in Christ, by which, in the one Spirit, we share in his filial relationship with the Father" (*Exploring Christology and Atonement*, 165; see further 131-166). The Western tradition tends to emphasize the "negative" aspect of the atonement, atonement *from* sin and death, but it often fails to emphasize the "positive" aspect, atonement for the sake of participation in the Triune God. Thus, Torrance writes:

The risen Jesus Christ is the living Atonement, atonement in its glorious achievement not only in overcoming the separation of sin, guilt and death, but in consummating union and communion with God in such a way that the divine life overflows freely through him into mankind.

— SPACE, TIME AND RESURRECTION, 55

For Torrance, the atonement is not yet complete until we consider its positive aspect, that of union and communion with God. It is incomplete if we only think in terms of its negative accomplishments (for example, when the doctrines of justification, expiation, propitiation, etc. become the focus). Both the positive and negative aspects are, of course, essential for the Gospel, but the emphasis should fall on the positive aspect of our communion with God rather than on the negative of our freedom from sin. The freedom we have in Christ is a freedom for the sake of communion with God, not merely freedom as an end in itself. Sin, guilt, death, and judgment were overcome *because* they kept us from union and communion with God. Without a firm understanding of this "*because*" we only understand half of the work of atonement.

This conviction results in a profound reconfiguration of the Gospel, in which we proclaim the unfathomable reality that "Our human nature is now set within the Father-Son relationship of Christ" (ibid., 69). This is the answer to the *why* of the Gospel, that we might share in the Son's fellowship with the Father in the communion of the Holy Spirit. If our understanding of the Gospel fails to proclaim this startling reality, then we proclaim an incomplete Gospel.

HOMOOUSION WITH US

The incarnation meant the humiliation of God to humanity, but it also meant the exaltation of human beings to the life of God. This begins with Christ's *homoousion,* not only with the Father in the Spirit but His oneness with us in our true humanity. This is the "divine exchange" described in 2 Corinthians 8:

For you know the generous act of our Lord Jesus Christ, that though he was rich, yet for your sakes he became poor, so that by his poverty you might become rich.

— NRSV, v. 9

Jesus Christ took up our impoverished humanity in order to heal our corrupt nature, put sin and death to death, and lift us up into the abounding wealth of God's Triune fellowship. Union with Christ begins with Christ's union with us. We have already discussed this with Torrance's conviction that Jesus assumed not merely a neutral human nature but a *fallen* one, truly *our* human nature. Christ must join us in our true state of being so that we might join Christ with God in God's state of being. If Christ's kinship with us is only partial, then our fellowship with God is only partial. If God has not assumed the whole of our existence, then our existence has not been embraced, healed, and redeemed for life in the Trinity. Accordingly, Torrance writes:

The *assumptio carnis* [assumption of flesh] means that God willed to *coexist* with the creature, that he the creator willed to exist also as a creature for the reconciliation of the estranged world to himself. Thus he the Lord of the covenant willed also to be its human partner in order to fulfil the covenant from its side. But this very condescension of God, in which he humbled himself to enter into our lowly creaturely and fallen existence, means also the elevation of our creaturely existence, by the very fact of God's will to unite himself to it and bring the creature into coexistence with himself. Thus his very act of becoming man is itself an act of reconciliation [...]

God has joined himself to us in our estranged human life in order to sanctify it, to gather it into union with his own holy life and so lift it up above and beyond all the downward drag of sin and decay, and that he already does simply by being one with man in all things. Thus the act of becoming incarnate is itself the *sanctification* of our human life in Jesus Christ, an elevating and fulfilling of it that far surpasses creation; it is a raising up of men and women to stand and have their being in the very life of God, but that raising up of man is achieved through his unutterable atoning self-humiliation and condescension.

— INCARNATION, 65-6

We are not united to Christ because we have done something to participate in the life of God but because God has come to us and participated *in our life*. This is why Torrance often marveled at the "sheer humanness" of Christ, "God sharing our hunger, thirst, tears, pain, and death [...] he does not override our humanity but completes, perfects, and establishes it" (*Preaching Christ Today,* 13). If God has truly become a human being in Christ, without ceasing to be God, then our human nature has been sanctified and lifted up into God's Triune life of love.

We have considered already the significance of the incarnation for Torrance's thought, but here we can see it in a better light as God's initiative to take up union with us in our human nature. God became one of us so that we might be united to Him and participate in the fellowship of God's being. Torrance applies the *homoousion* ("one in being") not only to the Son's oneness in being with the Father but also the Son's oneness in being *with us* in our frail humanity. This is why he writes, in the context of the Nicene Creed, "Both ends of the *homoousion,* the divine and the human, had to be secured. Everything would be emptied of evangelical and saving import if Jesus Christ were not fully, completely, entirely *man,* as well as *God*" (*The Trinitarian Faith,* 146).

This is reminiscent of a famous Patristic phrase that both Athanasius and Irenaeus echoed, "God became what we are in order to make us what He is Himself" (Athanasius, *On the Incarnation,* §54; Irenaeus, *Against Heresies,* book five). This remark has often been interpreted to mean the divinization or deification of human beings (that humans become gods), but Torrance rightly points out that this was never their original intent. The Patristics did not think that we become gods; this would only result in the dehumanization of our humanity. Christ did not come to make us any less human, but to heal our broken humanity. Torrance approvingly quotes George Florovsky, a prominent Eastern Orthodox theologian, who comments on this misunderstanding:

> The term *theosis* is indeed embarrassing, if we would think of it in 'ontological categories'. Indeed, man simply cannot become 'god'. But the Fathers were thinking in 'personal' terms, and the mystery of personal communion was involved at this point. Theosis means a personal encounter. It is the ultimate intercourse with God, in which the whole of human existence is, as it were, permeated by the Divine Presence.
>
> — FLOROVSKY: "ST GREGORY PALAMAS AND THE TRADITION OF THE FATHERS," 115; CITED IN TORRANCE: THE CHRISTIAN DOCTRINE OF GOD, 96

In agreement with Florovsky, Torrance thinks that Christ does not make us 'gods' in the sense that our *being* becomes divine. Instead, the Patristic Fathers were trying to express the fact that our personal life is so interpenetrated and united to the Triune God that we are taken up into the deepest of encounters in communion with God's eternal life. We do not "become god" but we are united with God in a personal union. The Patristics were struggling to express an inexpressible truth of the Gospel, one Western Christianity has almost entirely missed, the centrality of our union with Jesus Christ and through Him our participation in the Triune God.

This emphasis ultimately has the effect of refocusing our attention on the person of Jesus Christ. If we take seriously Torrance's conviction that union and participation, not merely atonement, is the goal of

Christ's life and work, then this would mean nothing less than a radical alteration in how we proclaim the Gospel today.

HUMANITY IN THE ASCENSION OF JESUS CHRIST

The importance of the true humanity of Jesus in the incarnation has often been stressed, but Torrance thinks it is just as important that we today stress His humanity in the *ascension*. Torrance considers this the new essential battle for theology, writing, "If in a previous generation we had to battle for the Humanity of the historical Jesus, today we have to do battle for the Humanity of the risen Jesus ascended to the right hand of God the Father Almighty" (*Royal Priesthood*, 43). The ascension is the astounding announcement that now and forever there is *a human being* in the heart of the Trinity. The incarnation did not end with the ascension but was fulfilled by it and continues from it. Jesus Christ remains now and forever a true human being, bone of our bone and flesh of our flesh, who mediates both the cause of God to humanity and the cause of humanity to God. Our hope for a new life with God is anchored in Jesus Christ's human participation in the Trinity.

This unique stress in Torrance's thought on the ascension is expressed by the Patristic doctrine of *theosis,* as Myk Habets writes:

> *Theosis* is the goal of all human existence, at the resurrection of body and soul human beings can fully participate in the eternal life of God. This participation always has one qualifier in Torrance's theology, however: it is participation in the eternal life of God *embodied in the incarnate Son.* There is no life without the Source of Life, no resurrection without the resurrected One, and no *theosis* outside of the incarnate Son of God. Thus *theosis* is not, strictly speaking, the 'divinisation' of the human person as such but the 'personalising' of the human being in *the* Person of the incarnate Son. This is the meaning behind the words of Torrance, 'for man to live in union with God is to become fully and perfectly human'.

Jesus alone is the *personalising Person* while we are *personalised persons.* It is from Christ alone, the one through whom creation came and the one for whom humanity was created, that men and women are radically made persons in the divine image.

— THEOSIS IN THE THEOLOGY OF THOMAS TORRANCE,

39

While Habets notes, "Direct references to *theosis* within Torrance's work are relatively few," it is important to recognize that "his work is significantly influenced by the conceptuality of it" (ibid., 14). Torrance's theology points strikingly towards this end. The human, bodily resurrection and ascension of Christ naturally correspond to *theosis,* in Torrance's usage of the word.

The ascension of Jesus Christ as a human being to the right hand of the Father was the humanization of humanity; it was not about humanity becoming divine. Thus Torrance writes, in terms of the resurrection, "The resurrection is the actualization of human reality, the humanizing in Jesus of dehumanized man" (*Space, Time and Resurrection,* 79). Participation in the life of God is the ultimate goal of humanity, not the end of humanity itself. Torrance's emphasis on *theosis* is centered around this humanization. We participate in God, in union with Jesus Christ, as He lives as a human being in *perichoresis* with the Father and the Holy Spirit. In and through Him we partake of the divine nature (2 Peter 1:4).

Union with Christ and participation through Him in the Triune life and love of God is the goal of the Gospel; this is what makes the Gospel truly "good news of great joy." It is not freedom from sin or an escape from hell alone but a human being participating in the life and love of God that is the goal of salvation and redemption, the heart of the Gospel. This explains why Torrance insisted on emphasized the humanity of Jesus in the ascension, as well as his implicit emphasis on the Patristic doctrine of *theosis.*

C. Baxter Kruger, a helpful interpreter of Torrance's thought, writes a clear summary of the importance of the ascension in the Gospel:

> Quite apart from our consultation or consent, the Son of God laid hold of the human race and decisively altered its very identity and existence. He took us down in his death. He crucified Adam, you, me, the human race, cleansed us of all alienation and converted us to his Father. He lifted us up in his resurrection, gave us new life, new birth—recreated us in the Holy Spirit. He exalted us in his ascension and took us home inside the circle of the very life and fellowship and joy and glory of the Triune God.
>
> — THE GREAT DANCE, KINDLE LOC. 965-8

The ascension means that God has laid hold of us and therefore, in union with Jesus Christ, that we have been included in the embrace of the Triune God. The very love that God is and has enjoyed from before all creation is our true home; it is where we belong. The ascension is our homecoming: Jesus has sought us out and lifted us up onto His shoulders like the one lost sheep. He has carried us home to enjoy the delight His Father's embrace (Luke 15).

In Christ's bodily resurrection we are made new, and in His ascension, we are included in the life and love of God. We are seated in heavenly places, as Paul wrote in Ephesians 2:

> But God, who is rich in mercy, out of the great love with which he loved us even when we were dead through our trespasses, made us alive together with Christ—by grace you have been saved—and raised us up with him and seated us with him in the heavenly places in Christ Jesus, so that in the ages to come he might show the immeasurable riches of his grace in kindness toward us in Christ Jesus.
>
> — NRSV, v. 4-7

Theological reflection on the ascension is often neglected, yet it is an essential aspect of the Gospel. Torrance's emphasis on Christ's ascension, and of us in Him, as well as his dedication to the original usage of *theosis,* forms the *capstone* of his theology.

ESCHATOLOGY

All of this does have an important "eschatological" tint to it that we must consider. Eschatology denotes the study of "last things," and in the Christian sense, it is the study of Christ's "second coming," or, more properly, his *parousia.* Torrance follows a common paradox when he discusses eschatology, which is sometimes known as the "now and not yet" tension. This is the tension between a realized eschatology, in which we have right now the benefits of redemption, and a futurist eschatology, in which we are waiting in expectation for the fullness of redemption. Thus Habets writes, "This participating in the Divine life (*theosis*) is an eschatological mystery that Torrance is careful not to delve into inappropriately. *Theosis* begins now as we participate in the new creation through the Spirit; it is also 'not yet' as we wait for the *Parousia* of the Lord when God in Christ will make all things new" (Theosis *in the Theology of Thomas Torrance,* 44). Torrance himself writes in terms of the ascension, "The ascension of Christ thus introduces, as it were, *an eschatological pause* in the heart of the *parousia* which makes it possible for us to speak of a first advent and a second or final advent of Christ" (*Space, Time and Resurrection,* 145). This eschatological pause is important to keep in mind whenever we are discussing the ascension or any other eschatological concept like it.

While it is important to stress our participation in the life of God as a reality we partake of *here and now,* there is an important eschatological expectation to it as well. We have the "down payment on our inheritance" (Eph. 1:14), but we do not yet have the fullness of God's coming Kingdom or the new creation of all things. We truly participate in the life of God, but we have not fully become the new (humanized) human beings in Christ. We are *hidden* together with Christ in

God (Col. 3:3). What it will all mean for us is something we cannot yet know, and vain speculation about this eschatological reality should be ruled out as altogether unhelpful. Union with Christ and participation in the life of God is a feast we partake of here and now by the Holy Spirit in us, but the fullness of this life with God is still yet to come.

PROPHET, PRIEST, AND KING BOTH NOW AND FOREVER

The continued relevance of the ascension should not be understated, even in the light of its coming fullness. The humanity of Jesus in the ascension not only *anchors* our hope in God's coming, but it means Christ acts both now and forever before the Father in continued mediation for us. We talk about the mediation of Jesus Christ on the Earth as our prophet, priest, and king (Calvin's doctrine of Christ's "threefold office"), however, we often fail to consider the *continued* mediation of Christ before the Father.

Not only in the past but also right now, Jesus Christ stands before the Father on behalf of all humanity as prophet, priest, and king. In Him, we are presented before God as "holy and blameless and irreproachable" (Col. 1:22). Logically this means that our worship, prayer, and faith is perfected in Him, as He prays, has faith, and communes with the Father on our behalf and in our name. Christ's vicarious humanity takes on a continued relevance for our lives because of the ascension. If Jesus' humanity was put to an end with the ascension, then we would have no lasting brotherhood with Christ. Therefore, we would have no lasting mediation before the Father. But Christ was not only a human being for us on Earth. Both now and forever Christ stands before the right hand of the Father in the Holy Spirit as a human being, and He acts vicariously for all humanity as one born of human flesh, as our brother. Torrance writes:

> In the humanity of the ascended Christ, there remains for ever before the Face of God the Father the one, perfect, sufficient Offering for

mankind. He presents himself before the Father as the Redeemer who has united himself to us and has become our Brother. He represents us before the Father as those who are incorporated in him and consecrated and perfected together with him in one for ever.

— SPACE, TIME AND RESURRECTION, 115

Furthermore, we can trace the ministry of the Church by the power of the Holy Spirit to Christ's ascension and continued mediation. As Christ's historical existence, the Church participates in *Christ's* ministry, and it does not establish its *own* independent ministry apart from Him. Christ's continued mediation before the Father is the basis for the Church's ministry on Earth, as Torrance writes, "Through the Spirit Christ's own priestly ministry is at work in and through the Church which is his body" (ibid., 115). The same is true for Christ's prophetic and kingly ministries, as the Word is proclaimed in the Church, and as the Church waits in hopeful expectation for His coming kingdom. (For more see Torrance, *Space, Time and Resurrection* 106-122; see also *Royal Priesthood.*)

MEETING GOD IN HIS PLACE

In the ascension, it was not Jesus *alone* who was lifted up to the right hand of the Father but also *us in Him.* Together with Christ we are included and embraced in the life and love of the Triune God, as we participate in the Son's relationship with the Father in the Holy Spirit. This follows Paul's logic in Colossians 3:

So if you have been raised with Christ, seek the things that are above, where Christ is, seated at the right hand of God. Set your minds on things that are above, not on things that are on earth, for you have died, and your life is hidden with Christ in God. When Christ who

is your life is revealed, then you also will be revealed with him
in glory.

— NRSV, v. 1-4

Where is our life? It is hidden in Him who sits at the right hand of the
Father, who participates, as a human being, by the Holy Spirit in
God's life, and who is there celebrated, embraced, and loved. Our true
life is in Him. Accordingly, Torrance writes:

> In the incarnation we have the meeting of man and God in man's
> place, but in the ascension we have the meeting of man and God in
> God's place

— SPACE, TIME AND RESURRECTION, 129

Jesus Christ assumed our fallen humanity, embracing us in our
corruption and sin so that we might meet God in God's place, being
made holy and sanctified in Christ. There is a definite downwards and
upwards movement to the Gospel, in which Christ meets us in our sin
in order to heal us and reconcile us to the Father. Without this
upwards movement, the Gospel is incomplete. Therefore, Torrance
writes:

> The ascension is the exaltation of new man, with his fully and truly
> human nature, and therefore of man with his 'place' as man, with the
> 'room' which he is given for his human life, to participation in the
> divine 'place', the 'place' which God makes by his own life, and the
> 'room' which he has for the fulfilment of his divine love. It is
> ascension in which our humanity in Christ is taken up into the full
> Communion of Father, Son and Holy Spirit in life and love.

— IBID., 133

Paul writes in 2 Corinthians 5 that all things have been made new in Christ. The new humanity in Him is not merely a sanctified and redeemed existence for its own sake, but it is sanctified and redeemed *so that* we may participate in the Triune life of God. As Torrance continues:

> The ascension means the exaltation of man into the life of God and on to the throne of God. In the ascension the Son of Man, New Man in Christ, is given to partake of divine nature. There we reach the goal of the incarnation, in our great *Prodomos* or Forerunner at the right hand of God. We are with Jesus beside God, for we are gather up in him and included in his own self-presentation before the Father.
>
> — Ibid., 135

This is the stunning conclusion of Torrance's theology, the goal to which it all points: *we are with Jesus beside God.* We are lifted up and included in the life and love of the Holy Trinity. Our humanity is not brushed aside, because in Him it fulfills its ultimate purpose, communion with God. This is the *capstone* of Torrance's theology: in union with Jesus Christ, made new by His death and resurrection and lifted up into the life of God, we participate in the love of the Holy Trinity —we are with Jesus beside God.

SIDEBAR: RESURRECTION

In chapter nine, we have emphasized the human ascension of Jesus Christ, but it will also be important to consider the nature of the resurrection event briefly. The two events are connected, and Torrance often talked about them in the same breath. The resurrection is, however, unique in itself. Theologically, it denotes our being raised to a new life together with Christ, but there is an important consideration to be made about the *nature* of this event. Torrance describes the resurrection in the following way:

> The resurrection of Jesus is an event that happens within history in continuity with the living event of the whole historical existence of Jesus, yet as an event of fulfilled redemption the resurrection issues in a new creation beyond the corruptible processes of this world, on the other side of decay and death, and on the other side of judgement, in the fullness of a new world and of a new order of things.
>
> — SPACE, TIME AND RESURRECTION, 86

From this we can deduce a classical understanding of the resurrection as 1) bodily and 2) historical, but we also sense Torrance's insightful contribution, in which the resurrection is 3) *a new kind of historical happening.*

1. *Bodily resurrection.* Torrance strongly affirms the resurrection of Jesus Christ as a *bodily* resurrection. He writes sharply, "Everything depends on the resurrection of the body, otherwise all we have is a Ghost for a Saviour" (ibid., 87).

2. *Historical resurrection.* In order for the resurrection event to have an effect on *our* world, on human beings in space and time, it must be a historical event. Thus Torrance writes, "If the resurrection is not an event in history, a happening within the same order of physical existence to which we belong, then atonement and redemption are empty vanities, for they achieve nothing for historical men and women in the world" (ibid.).

3. *The resurrection is a new kind of historical happening.* The central thing to consider, however, is that while the resurrection was bodily and historical, it was, at the same time, *more than* bodily or historical. It cannot be reduced to biological consequences, nor can it be limited to the restraints of human history (in which it might have its content discovered by historical investigation). The resurrection means that the historical and bodily existence of humanity was recapitulated and redeemed. It is not an event totally accessible to human historical examination; it was not a human event but a divine event *in* human history. It must be considered as *more than merely historical fact* since it was God's gracious redemption of history and of bodily humanity. The resurrection "bursts through the structures and limitations of space and time as we know them" (ibid., 88).

It is necessary for the resurrection to be at once a historical event in space and time, and yet more than a historical event, in order for the resurrection to be the divine redemption of human beings. Torrance writes at length:

> If those patterns of our existence, conditioned and determined by sin
> and guilt, remain rigid and hard, if Christ has not broken through

them and opened a way for new being beyond them, he cannot be *our* redeemer, for we cannot be separated from that space-time existence of ours in this world. But if he is the Redeemer who does deliver us from the thraldom [slavery] of sin and guilt and therefore breaks through the structures determined by them to which we are subjected, then the resurrection event is not something that can be caught within the framework of those structures or interpreted by the secular historian who can only work within it [...] As happening within this kind of time, and as event within this kind of history, the resurrection, by being what it is, resists and overcomes corruption and decay, and is therefore, a *new kind of historical happening* which instead of tumbling down into the grave and oblivion rises out of the death of what is past into continuing being and reality. This is temporal happening that runs not backwards but forwards, and overcomes all illusion and privation or being. This is fully real historical happening, so real that it remains real happening and does not slip away from us, but keeps pace with us and outruns us as we tumble down in decay and lapse into death and the dust of past history and even comes to meet us out of the future. That is how we are to think of the risen Christ Jesus. He is not dead but alive, more real than any of us.

— Ibid., 88-9

As a new kind of historical happening, the resurrection means the redemption of history and of historical persons from corruption and death into the life of God. This is the true meaning of God's "eternity." It is not timelessness but true time, the time which does not destroy or end in death but continually adds life to life. The redemption of history from corruption is included in the brand new historical event of the resurrection. Therefore, Torrance writes, "[T]he resurrection means the *redemption of space and time*" (ibid., 90). Space and time are not "abrogated or transcended," but "healed and restored, just as our being is healed and restored through the resurrection" (ibid.). This is how Torrance understands the resurrection. It should not be considered a purely historical event, nor should it be considered purely theologically. As Torrance writes, "[W]e can interpret the resurrection only if we interpret it theologically as well as historically" (ibid., 94). It is at once historical and theological, taking place in history without being limited by history.

THE LIFE OF JESUS CHRIST

Torrance applies his understanding of the resurrection to the life of Jesus Christ, calling the resurrection the "key to the bewildering enigma of Jesus," which "provides [...] a structure consistent with the whole [of Christ's life]" (*Space, Time and Resurrection*, 164). We do not merely interpret Christ's life historically, but we also have to consider it theologically. Thus, "Jesus remains live and a real historical happening, more real and more historical than any other historical event" (ibid., 95). As Paul recognized, Jesus Christ came in the "fullness of time" (Gal. 4:4). Like the resurrection, Jesus Himself is historical, yet He is at once a new kind of historical event.

Neither a purely historical nor a purely theological doctrine of Christ is sufficient. This has important ramifications to the so-called "quest for the historical Jesus." According to Torrance, there is no purely historical Jesus free from all theological considerations, and to imply as much would be to lean towards the Ebionite heresy, in which Christ is only seen as human and not divine. Likewise, Christ's life cannot be considered purely "theological" and without history, as in Rudolf Bultmann's demythologizing program, in which Christ is stripped of historical content. Both the theological and historical must be held together. This is what the resurrection informs us about the life of Jesus, as Torrance writes, "[T]he resurrection is to be understood in consistency with Jesus Christ himself" (*Space, Time and Resurrection*, 94). In the light of the resurrection, we can rightly understand Christ's life in space and time.

Good news

What the resurrection ultimately means for the Church today, beyond all these rather technical considerations, is that our message is not one of doom and gloom but of bountiful hope and joy. We proclaim the truly *good* news of resurrection, not of death or annihilation. Torrance brings out this emphasis well:

The Church of the risen Lord has no right to be a prophet of gloom or despair, for this world has been redeemed and sanctified by Christ, and he will not let it go. The corruptible clay of our poor earth has been taken up in Jesus, is consecrated through his sacrifice and resurrection, and he will not allow it to sink back into corruption. Hence the whole creation groans and travails waiting for the manifestation of the sons of God, looking forward with eager expectation to the hour of final liberation and renewal in the advent of its risen Saviour. The Church must learn to take into its mouth the Good News of the resurrection and new creation, for that must be its primary note, one of limitless joy and thanksgiving [...] The involvement of the Church in the suffering of mankind must never be allowed to stifle that supreme note of resurrection triumph or to smother the eschatological joy at the astounding events that have broken into history and pledged for mankind the final day of regeneration.

— Space, Time and Resurrection, 105

In the next chapter, we will draw this book to a close by reflecting on this important reminder. Torrance calls us today, in the light of the resurrection, to proclaim the Gospel as truly *good* news of great joy.

CONCLUSION: HOW TO PREACH THE GOSPEL

Torrance's theology provides the means for a radical revision to the way we preach the Gospel today. Personally, this is perhaps the greatest lesson I have learned from Torrance's theology, so it seems fitting to end this book with a reflection on how Torrance helps us preach the Gospel rightly. Instead of preaching a message of "doom and gloom," where the burden of salvation is thrown upon the shoulders of sinners unable to "rightly respond" to God's grace, Torrance compels us to proclaim the message of God's truly unconditional grace and love. Torrance writes at length:

> There is, then, an evangelical way to preach the Gospel and an unevangelical way to preach it. The Gospel is preached in an unevangelical way, as happens so often in modern evangelism, when the preacher announces: This is what Jesus Christ has done for you, but you will not be saved *unless* you make your own personal decision for Christ as your Saviour. Or: Jesus Christ loved you and gave his life for you on the Cross, but you will be saved only *if* you give your heart to him. In that event what is actually coming across

to people is not a Gospel of unconditional grace but some other Gospel of conditional grace which belies the essential nature and content of the Gospel as it is in Jesus... To preach the Gospel in that conditional or legalist way has the effect of telling poor sinners that in the last resort the responsibility for their salvation is taken off the shoulders of the Lamb of God and placed upon them—but in that case they feel that they will never be saved [...]

How, then, is the Gospel to be preached in a genuinely evangelical way? Surely in such a way that full and central place is given to *the vicarious humanity of Jesus* as the all-sufficient human response to the saving love of God which he has freely and unconditionally provided for us. We preach and teach the Gospel evangelically, then, in such a way as this: God loves you so utterly and completely that he has given himself for you in Jesus Christ his beloved Son, and has thereby pledged his very Being as God for your salvation. In Jesus Christ God has actualised his unconditional love for you in your human nature in such a once for all way, that he cannot go back upon it without undoing the Incarnation and the Cross and thereby denying himself. Jesus Christ died for you precisely because you are sinful and utterly unworthy of him, and has thereby already made you his own before and apart from your ever believing in him. He has bound you to himself by his love in a way that he will never let you go, for even if you refuse him and damn yourself in hell his love will never cease. Therefore, repent and believe in Jesus Christ as your Lord and Saviour. From beginning to end what Jesus Christ has done for you he has done not only as God but as man. He has acted in your place in the whole range of your human life and activity, including your personal decisions, and your responses to God's love, and even your acts of faith. He has believed for you, fulfilled your human response to God, even made your personal decision for you, so that he acknowledges you before God as one who has already responded to God in him, who has already believed in God through him, and whose personal decision is already implicated in Christ's self-offering to the Father, in all of which he has been fully and completely accepted by the Father, so that in Jesus Christ you are already accepted by him. Therefore, renounce yourself, take up your cross and follow Jesus as your Lord and Saviour.

— THE MEDIATION OF CHRIST, 93-4

What strikes me the most about this presentation is the sheer *objective* nature of its message, and yet, it is an objectivity without the loss of personal subjectivity in responding through the vicarious humanity of Christ. The Gospel announcement is not a *possibility* of what might happen if we believe enough; it is the statement of a fact, truly *the* fact of all existence. The Gospel is not a good *opportunity;* it is good *news.* It takes on the character of an *announcement,* not a *sales pitch.*

Torrance balances well the sheer objectivity of the Gospel without leaving behind the subjective element. He makes room for the sinner to respond in faith and repentance (through Christ's vicarious faith and repentance on our behalf). Repentance does not *change* reality but *sees* reality rightly. The good news is the truth of our existence even *before* we believe it; repentance simply means a "change of mind," in which we learn to see and accept the Gospel's announcement as the fundamental truth of our existence and live according to its truth. If we are to preach the Gospel again today as God's unconditional grace, then we must stress Christ's life lived on our behalf, and only then our personal responses made within His vicarious response.

> To preach the Gospel of the unconditional grace of God in that unconditional way is to set before people the astonishingly good news of what God has freely provided for us in the vicarious humanity of Jesus. To repent and believe in Jesus Christ and commit myself to him on that basis means that I do not need to look over

my shoulder all the time to see whether I have really given myself personally to him, whether I really believe and trust him, whether my faith is at all adequate, for in faith it is not upon my faith, my believing or my personal commitment that I rely, but solely upon what Jesus Christ has done for me, in my place and on my behalf, and what he is and always will be as he stands in for me before the face of the Father. That means that I am completely liberated from all ulterior motives in believing or following Jesus Christ, for on the ground of his vicarious human response for me, I am free for spontaneous joyful response and worship and service as I could not otherwise be.

— IBID., 94-5

Torrance recalls a conversation he had shortly after being nominated to the office of Moderator of the General Assembly of the Church of Scotland. A member asked if he was "born again." Naturally, Torrance said yes, he was; but when the man asked, "When were you born again?", Torrance made this stunning reply:

I still recall his face when I told him that I had been born again when Jesus Christ was born of the Virgin Mary and rose again from the virgin tomb, the first-born from the dead. When he asked me to explain I said: 'This Tom Torrance you see is full of corruption, but the real Tom Torrance is hid with Christ in God and will be revealed only when Jesus Christ comes again. He took my corrupt humanity in his Incarnation, sanctified, cleansed and redeemed it, giving it new birth, in his death and resurrection.' In other words, our new birth, our regeneration, our conversion, are what has taken place in Jesus Christ himself, so that when we speak of our conversion or our regeneration we are referring to our sharing in the conversion or regeneration of our humanity brought about by Jesus in and through himself for our sake. In a profound and proper sense, therefore, we must speak of Jesus Christ as constituting himself the very substance of our conversion, so that we must think of him as taking our place even in our acts of repentance and personal decision, for without him all so-called repentance and conversion are empty.

— IBID., 86

The Church today has much to learn from Torrance, and perhaps the most important lesson of all, in my opinion, is this radical renewal of the Gospel. Reading Torrance has shaped my understanding of the Gospel profoundly. I was once upon a time a "fundamentalist" screaming doom and gloom instead of the good news of God's love. I remember my high school days of "street evangelism." I would walk up to a stranger and ask them a series of condemning questions: "Have you ever lied? You're a liar. Have you ever stolen something, even a paperclip? You're a thief. You've broken two of God's commandments, which means you're a sinner and God's fiery wrath is on you. You deserve hell."

Only at this point would I explain the "good news" that Jesus died to save you from His angry Father and the hell He wants to send you to forever. It was a technique designed to shame and guilt sinners until they agreed to say the magic words we call the "sinners prayer." But this stems from a failure to understand the Gospel as truly good news. I only understood the negative side of the Gospel and never fully grasped myself why we called it good news to begin with.

Thankfully, the Gospel is not so gloomy. I thought I knew it so well in those days, but Torrance opened my eyes to see the good news as truly *good* news. It is not the message of hell or sin or wrath, but of love, grace, mercy, and the beauty of all Christ has done and is doing still for us today. The Gospel is not a "basic" truth of the Christian life, from which we must "grow up" in Christ and move onto more important subjects. May we today come to see the Gospel again as truly good news, and may we proclaim it to the world as such.

When the Church catches a fresh glimpse of what makes the good news truly *good* news, we will once again have a message to proclaim that will turn the world upside down. This is what I believe Torrance's theology helps us with the most because it is what has helped me the most.

A BRIEF READING GUIDE

Here you will find the resources I recommend for further reading. This is not an exhaustive list of the books either written by Torrance or about him, but these are the books I have found helpful in studying his theology. I list them here in the order I found them to be the most valuable or relevant.

Books written by Torrance are listed as either "introductory," "evangelical," or "scientific" books. The introductory books are those I recommend for newcomers to Torrance, the books I consider to be his most accessible. The "evangelical" books are those dealing directly with Christian doctrines such as the Trinity, incarnation, and atonement. The point here isn't to divide up Torrance's thought; his work actively resists such a neat division. However, Torrance's books tend to fall into one of these two categories, either with an emphasis on Christian doctrines or on the scientific method of theology. The "scientific" books, therefore, focus more directly on Torrance's scientific theology, though of course, they are not completely free from evangelical content.

I have purposefully excluded any of Torrance's many published essays from this list. It is not because these essays are of no importance (they are extremely important), but because these are rarely available to laymen without academic connections to the journals they were published in. Those essays that have been republished into books are, of course, listed, but individual essays have been excluded on account of their limited availability.

INTRODUCTORY BOOKS:

The Mediation of Christ - This is one of my favorite books by Torrance, if not my favorite. It is an accessible little book that addresses many of the major themes from his work. Make sure you read the second edition, which includes an important final chapter on the Trinity in the atonement.

Preaching Christ Today - This short book strikes right to the heart of Torrance's theology by focusing on his passion for the Gospel.

A Passion for Christ - This is a collection of essays from the three Torrance brothers: James, Thomas, and David. Thomas wrote the first two chapters, and they offer a clear and concise introduction to his theology.

Christian Theology and Scientific Culture - I found this book to be the most accessible of Torrance's "scientific" books, and I recommend it since it contains, in clear terms, many of his core convictions in this area.

"EVANGELICAL" BOOKS:

Incarnation: The Person and Life of Christ

Atonement: The Person and Work of Christ - These volumes were published after Torrance's death and originate from his lectures on Christology at New College, Edinburgh. Robert T. Walker (Torrance's nephew) has edited these exceptionally well. He provides many helpful footnotes, introductions, and appendixes for each volume. They are perhaps the closest thing available to a systematic theology written by Torrance.

The Christian Doctrine of God - This is arguably Torrance's most important book. It was one he wrote later in life, after being unable to teach the doctrine of God for many years. It's a stunning presentation of the doctrine of the Trinity, but also a prime sampling of Torrance's overall thought. It's one of the best books of theology I've ever read.

The Trinitarian Faith - This is a detailed examination of the Nicene Creed. It contains a good deal of Patristic scholarship, but it is marked with Torrance's own particular insights. Torrance called this book his favorite from the ones he had written.

Reality and Evangelical Theology - This book contains important insights into Torrance's "critically realist" approach to theology, his understanding of the bible and divine revelation. An important "epistemological" or "methodological" book.

Space, Time and Resurrection - An important collection of essays on the resurrection and ascension of Christ.

Theology in Reconstruction - Another valuable collection of essays, covering subjects such as the knowledge of God, reformed theology, the doctrine of justification, and the Holy Spirit.

Theology in Reconciliation - This book engages in an ecumenical dialogue between the Eastern and Western Churches. It contains excellent work on the sacraments.

Scottish Theology from John Knox to John McLeod Campbell - Another one of Torrance's self-proclaimed favorites from the books he wrote; this is the culmination of Torrance's lifelong engagement with Scottish theology.

When Christ Comes and Comes Again

The Apocalypse Today - These two books contain some of Torrance's published sermons from his time as a pastor.

Conflict and Agreement in the Church (two volumes) - This is a collection of essays that originated from Torrance's engagement with the ecumenical movement.

Trinitarian Perspectives - The culmination of Torrance's ecumenical dialogue with the Orthodox Church on a joint agreement on the doctrine of the Trinity.

Divine Interpretation - An insightful collection, recently published, on the study of hermeneutics in both modern and medieval theologians. It reprints Torrance's important essay, "Karl Barth and the Latin Heresy."

Royal Priesthood - A helpful book on the ministry of the Church in the light of Christ's royal priesthood.

Karl Barth: An Introduction to His Early Theology - A classic study of Barth's early theology from 1910-1931. Though the focus is on Barth's thought, this is an insightful book for understanding Torrance's own work as well.

Karl Barth: Biblical and Evangelical Theologian - This volume collects some of Torrance's best essays on Karl Barth's theology, though it is sadly out of print.

Calvin's Doctrine of Man - Torrance was also a noted scholar in John Calvin's theology and helped oversee the translation of his commentaries into English (together with his brother, David).

"Scientific" books:

Theological Science - This book established Torrance's reputation as an expert in the dialogue of science and theology. He won the Templeton prize for this book, and it contains his most extensive treatment of theological science.

God and Rationality - The sequel to *Theological Science,* this book explores more of the relationship between natural science and theological science. I found it to be one of the most helpful resources for understanding Torrance clearly on a number of issues, including those not limited to his scientific thought.

Reality and Scientific Theology - Essential for understanding Torrance's scientific theology, especially his "reformulated" or "new" natural theology.

Space, Time and Incarnation - Torrance explores the concepts of space and time in the movement of thought from "container" notions to "relational" notions.

Transformation & Convergence in the Frame of Knowledge - Many indispensable essays on science and theology are collected in this book, some of which were especially helpful for understanding Torrance's reformulated natural theology.

The Ground and Grammar of Theology - Another insightful look at Torrance's scientific approach, with many helpful remarks on the Trinity as the ground and grammar of theological knowledge in connection with Torrance's stratification of knowledge model.

Divine and Contingent Order - Torrance admitted that this book was written more for scientists than theologians, but it is fascinating for precisely that reason.

The Christian Frame of Mind - A short but helpful book. Look for the second edition (Wipf & Stock) with an introduction by W. Jim Neidhardt.

AUDIO LECTURES:

A large number of T. F. Torrance's audio recordings are freely available online. These are exceptionally helpful. You can find some of these recordings compiled at the following links:

http://moltmanniac.com/thomas-f-torrance-audio-lectures/

https://www.gci.org/av/tftaudio

SECONDARY SOURCES:

The Promise of Trinitarian Theology edited by Elmer M. Colyer. The essays in this collection were written by prominent theologians and scholars of Torrance's theology, and Torrance himself writes a response to each essay.

How to Read T.F. Torrance by Elmer M. Colyer. This is the go-to book for an overview of Torrance's theology, and it is the most complete guide written to date.

T.F. Torrance: An Intellectual Biography by Alister E. McGrath. The most complete biography of Torrance written so far, with a special interest in the development of Torrance's thought.

Exploring Christology and Atonement by Andrew Purves. This book includes extensive treatment of Torrance alongside two important influences on his thought: H.R. Mackintosh and John McLeod Campbell. The chapter on Torrance's doctrine of atonement is excellent, clear, and one of the most helpful I've read.

Theology in Transposition by Myk Habets. An excellent book on Torrance by one of the leading scholars of his theology.

Theosis in the Theology of Thomas Torrance by Myk Habets. A classic study focusing on Torrance's usage of *theosis*.

Thomas F. Torrance: Theologian of the Trinity by Paul D. Molnar. A thorough and insightful treatment of Torrance's Trinitarian theology. This book covers a lot of ground and is perhaps one of the best introductions to Torrance for those willing to put in the work.

Participatio: Journal of the Thomas F. Torrance Theological Fellowship. This is an ongoing academic journal dedicated to Torrance's theology. You can freely access each volume on the fellowship's website: www.tftorrance.org. These volumes contain many insightful essays on Torrance's work from a wide range of scholarly sources.

Trinitarian Grace and Participation by Geordie W. Ziegler. By focusing on the themes of grace and participation in Torrance's thought, this book provides a great overview of Torrance's theology.

Encountering Reality by Travis M. Stevick. This is a careful treatment of Torrance's usage of *kata physin* in dialogue with modern science and philosophy. Insightful for those wanting to dive deeper into this idea and how it relates to the larger field of epistemology.

C. Baxter Kruger's books have "popularized" many of Torrance's insights, making his central convictions accessible to a larger audience. See especially *The Shack Revisited, Across All Worlds, The Great Dance,* and *Jesus and the Undoing of Adam.* Kruger's work was my introduction to Torrance.

An Introduction to Torrance Theology edited by Gerrit Scott

Dawson. This volume includes essays from leading scholars on all three of the Torrance brother's theological contributions.

Worship, Community and the Triune God of Grace by James B. Torrance. While this is not a book directly on Torrance, it is a profound book of a similar focus, written by his brother.

Flesh and Blood by Daniel J. Cameron. A short but helpful book for navigating the controversy surrounding the notion that Jesus Christ assumed a fallen nature. It is clearly written and explores Torrance's treatment of the subject at length.

Persons in Communion by Alan J. Torrance. Alan is the Son of James B. Torrance. This book develops upon Torrance's Trinitarian theology in a fascinating way.

Face to Face (vol. 1-3) by Marty Folsom. Marty is one of the most well-read scholars I know, and his series presents many important theological insights in clear and accessible language. While he does not directly explore Torrance's thought, it is apparent that Torrance's influence on his work is strong.

WORKS CITED

Works cited are listed in order of appearance, by chapter, and have not been repeated by sequential use.

Introduction:

Participatio: The Journal of the Thomas F. Torrance Theological Fellowship, Vol. 1 2009. Accessed digitally: http://www.tftorrance.org/journal/participatio_vol_1_2009.pdf
Exploring Christology and Atonement: Conversations with John McLeod Campbell, H. R. Mackintosh and T. F. Torrance by Andrew Purves. InterVarsity Press, 2015.
Theology in Reconstruction by Thomas F. Torrance. SCM Press LTD, 1965.

Biography:

T.F. Torrance: An Intellectual Biography by Alister E. McGrath. T&T Clark, 1999.

The Promise of Trinitarian Theology edited by Elmer M. Colyer. Rowman & Littlefield Publishers, Inc., 2001.

The Doctrine of Jesus Christ: The Auburn Lectures 1938-39 by Thomas F. Torrance. Wipf and Stock Publishers, 2002.

Chapter 1:

Space, Time and Resurrection by Thomas F. Torrance. Wm. B. Eerdmans Publishing, 1976.

Reality and Evangelical Theology by Thomas F. Torrance. The Westminster Press, 1982.

Theology in Transposition: A Constructive Appraisal of T.F. Torrance by Myk Habets. Fortress Press, 2013.

God and Rationality by Thomas F. Torrance. T&T Clark, 1997.

Christian Theology and Scientific Culture by Thomas F. Torrance. Oxford University Press, 1981.

The Ground and Grammar of Theology by Thomas F. Torrance. Christian Journals Limited, 1980.

Reality and Scientific Theology by Thomas F. Torrance. Wipf and Stock Publishers, 1985.

Theological Science by Thomas F. Torrance. Oxford University Press, 1969.

How to Read T.F. Torrance by Elmer M. Colyer. InterVarsity Press, 2001.

Chapter 2:

Preaching Christ Today: The Gospel and Scientific Thinking by Thomas F. Torrance. Wm. B. Eerdmans Publishing, 1994.

"The Stratification of Knowledge in the Thought of T.F. Torrance" by Benjamin Myers. First published in the *Scottish Journal of Theology* vol. 61 issue 1, February 2008, pages 1-15.

Dietrich Bonhoeffer Works Volume 11 by Dietrich Bonhoeffer. Fortress Press, 2001.

Chapter 3:

Church Dogmatics by Karl Barth. 14 vol. edited by G. W. Bomiley and T. F. Torrance. T&T Clark, 2004.

Transformation & Convergence in the Frame of Knowledge: Explorations in the Interrelations of Scientific and Theological Enterprise by Thomas F. Torrance. Wipf and Stock Publishers, 1984.

Thomas F. Torrance: Theologian of the Trinity by Paul D. Molnar. Ashgate Publishing, 2009.

Chapter 4:

The Mediation of Christ by Thomas F. Torrance. Helmer & Howard Publishers, 1992.

The Trinitarian Faith: The Evangelical Theology of the Ancient Catholic Church by Thomas F. Torrance. T&T Clark, 2016.

A Passion for Christ: The Vision that Ignites Ministry by Thomas F. Torrance, James B. Torrance, and David W. Torrance. Wipf and Stock Publishers, 2010.

The Christian Doctrine of God by Thomas F. Torrance. T&T Clark, 2001.

Incarnation: The Person and Life of Christ by Thomas F. Torrance; ed. Robert T. Walker. InterVarsity Press, 2008.

Atonement: The Person and Work of Christ by Thomas F. Torrance; ed. Robert T. Walker. InterVarsity Press, 2009.

"Universalism or Election" by Thomas F. Torrance in *Scottish Journal of Theology* 1949, pp 310-318.

Institutes of the Christian Religion by John Calvin; trans. Henry Beveridge. Accessed digitally: http://www.ccel.org/ccel/calvin/institutes.

Chapter 5:

The Trinity by Karl Rahner. Bloomsbury Publishing, 2001.

On the Trinity by St. Augustine. This work is in the public domain.

The School of Faith: The Catechisms of the Reformed Church translated and edited with an introduction by Thomas F. Torrance. The Camelot Press Ltd., 1959.

Trinitarian Perspectives: Towards Doctrinal Agreement by Thomas F. Torrance. T&T Clark, 1994.

Chapter 6:

Theology in Reconciliation by Thomas F. Torrance. Geoffrey Chapman Publishers, 1975.

Chapter 7:

Worship, Community and the Triune God of Grace by James B. Torrance. InterVarsity Press, 1997.

Trinitarian Grace and Participation: An Entry into the Theology of T.F. Torrance by Geordie W. Ziegler. Fortress Press, 2017.

Flesh and Blood: A Dogmatic Sketch Concerning the Fallen Nature View of Christ's Human Nature by Daniel J. Cameron. Wipf and Stock Publishers, 2016.

Chapter 8:

Christus Victor: An Historical Study of the Three Main Types of the Idea of the Atonement by Gustaf Aulén. Wipf and Stock Publishers reprint, 2003.

On the Incarnation by St. Athanasius.

Atonement, Justice, and Peace: The Message of the Cross and the Mission of the Church by Darrin W. Snyder Belousek. Wm. B. Eerdmans Publishing, 2011.

"The Atoning Obedience of Christ" by Thomas F. Torrance. Moravian Theological Seminary Bulletin, 1959.

Divine Interpretation by Thomas F. Torrance; ed. Adam Nigh and Todd Speidell. Wipf and Stock Publishers, 2017.

Chapter 9:

Royal Priesthood: A Theology of Ordained Ministry by Thomas F. Torrance. T&T Clarck, 2000.

Theosis in the Theology of Thomas Torrance by Myk Habets. Routledge, 2016.

The Great Dance: The Christian Vision Revisited by C. Baxter Kruger. Perichoresis Press, 2011.

ABOUT THE AUTHOR

STEPHEN D. MORRISON is a prolific American writer, ecumenical theologian, novelist, artist, and literary critic. A strong sense of creativity and curiosity drives his productive output of books on a wide range of subjects.

This book is the third in his "Plain English Series." Previous volumes include *Karl Barth in Plain English* and *T. F. Torrance in Plain English*.

For more on Stephen, please visit his website. There you can stay up to date with his latest projects and ongoing thoughts.

WWW.SDMORRISON.ORG

ALSO BY STEPHEN D. MORRISON

Printed in Great Britain
by Amazon